THE GOSPEL *in the* GLOBAL VILLAGE

—◈ *Seeking God's Dream of Shalom* ◈—

Katharine Jefferts Schori

Morehouse Publishing
NEW YORK · HARRISBURG · DENVER

Unless otherwise noted, the Scripture quotations contained herein are from the New Revised Standard Version Bible, copyright © 1989 by the Division of Christian Education of the National Council of Churches of Christ in the U.S.A. Used by permission. All rights reserved.

Morehouse Publishing, 4775 Linglestown Road, Harrisburg, PA 17112

Morehouse Publishing, 445 Fifth Avenue, New York, NY 10016

Morehouse Publishing is an imprint of Church Publishing Incorporated

Cover design by Christina Hope

Library of Congress Cataloging-in-Publication Data

Jefferts Schori, Katharine.
    The Gospel in the global village : seeking God's dream of shalom / Katharine Jefferts Schori.
        p.   cm.
    Includes bibliographical references (p.   ) and index.
    ISBN 978-0-8192-2343-2 (pbk. : alk. paper)
    1. Episcopal Church. 2. Speeches, addresses, etc. I. Title.
BX5937.J44G67   2009
252'.0373—dc22
                                                        2009011879

Printed in the United States of America

09 10 11 12 13 14   10 9 8 7 6 5 4 3 2 1

to Kate and Aaron,
whose faithfulness and
hope are an inspiration to their elders

Contents

Foreword

This collection is a sampling of the work I do in speaking good news, encouraging, and challenging Episcopalians around the church and people of other traditions (and none). Together, we can partner to build a world that is more godly and more humane—a holy, whole, and healed place for all God's creatures.

Acknowledgments

This book would not have been possible without the support of many others. I am exceedingly grateful to Nancy Fitzgerald, editor and nudge, whose persistence brought this collection to print. I give thanks to and for my remarkable staff, who keep me moving around the global village and keep the office running while I am on the road: Chuck Robertson, right hand and far more accomplished author than I; Sharon Jones, who makes all the arrangements for the traveling, preaching, and speaking; Miguel Escobar, who keeps up with the mountains of correspondence; Ednice Baerga, who helps keep track of the part of my work having to do with fellow bishops; and finally, Linda Watt, who looks after all the staff of the Episcopal Church Center and keeps us moving in creative and faithful directions. I could not do the work I do without the support of my husband of nearly 30 years—Dick, the rock climber who first invited me into the mysteries of tiny, nearly invisible handholds and the majesty of summits. Much spiritual wisdom is to be found on those rocks.

PART ONE

CITY OF GOD

The City on a Hill

Little Rock, Arkansas, USA
Clinton School of Public Service
6 January 2007

This speech was given to an informal gathering of the school's fellows and those intent on serving the wider society. It was followed by a wide-ranging conversation with the audience.

I applaud the focus of the Clinton School of Public Service on training and educating leaders for global service, and seeking equity for all. Those are great and noble aims. When leaders hold out a large and ambitious vision, the result is passion for that vision—and the possibility of achieving it. This school builds on a heritage of those who have sought to exemplify that kind of lofty vision.

We have this week buried a man who worked from a large and ambitious vision. While Gerald Ford had less time than many others in the position for which he is best remembered, his funeral reminded us all of the need for healing the hurts and ills in this world. His act of pardon, unwelcome in some quarters at the time, brought this nation healing, and he himself paid the price. Mercy is not altogether a popular virtue. But the compassionate urge toward healing—and healing for the whole world—is what motivates mercy.

That deep sense of righting the wrongs and injustices of this world is needed in ever-increasing abundance. We need creative and compassionate leaders who can help to find healing in Darfur and the Middle East—we need them today, as we needed them in Ireland and South Africa in the 1980s and '90s. There will be equally deep need in human communities as you leave this place and move into your work.

The search for equity—the basic dignity of each human being—underlies many of the world's great religious traditions, especially those with which this part of the world is most familiar. The three Abrahamic faiths—Judaism, Christianity, and Islam—seek a broad vision of peace with justice, known as *shalom* or *salaam*. Judaism embraces the great visions of the prophet Isaiah, of a banquet spread on a hillside, of a city set on a hill to which all the nations will come. Those visions take flesh in a community where the hungry are fed, the ill are healed, prisoners are set free, the blind have their sight restored, and the poor hear good news about liberation from oppression.

Jesus' first reported act of public ministry, in the Gospel of Luke, is to read from that vision of Isaiah's, and to say, "Today this scripture has been fulfilled in your hearing" (Luke 4:21). In doing so, he claims that vision as his own. Christians seek to make that scripture reality in this day as well.

Islam draws its very name from the understanding that peace comes in submitting to the will of God, in living in right relationship to God and other human beings. *Islam, shalom,* and *salaam* all have the same root in a word that means a good deal more than simply "peace."

That vision of peace with justice, where no one oppresses the poor, where all are able to live at liberty, where no one's God-given potential is limited because of unchosen accidents of birth or life—gender, race, class, disability, illness—lies behind the work of prophetic leaders. Prophetic leaders, which I desperately hope you are becoming, are those who can dream big dreams of a world restored, and challenge the political systems of our day to move toward those dreams.

In our day, that vision of a world restored, a world where the poorest have enough to eat and access to education, health care, and the basic necessities of dignified human life, is exemplified in the United Nations Millennium Development Goals. The goals are a concrete vision of the possible, achievable by the year 2015, and include:

- feeding the one-third of the world's people who go to bed hungry each night

- providing primary education for girls as well as boys

- improving maternal health care

- reducing childhood mortality rates

- preventing and treating AIDS, tuberculosis, malaria, and other diseases

- working toward gender equity and the empowerment of women

- ensuring environmentally sustainable development

- building global partnerships for development, with a focus on debt, aid, and trade

These goals frame a bold but achievable vision that challenges all the peoples and governments of the world. To reach those goals, the developed nations will need to increase their giving to development work—and the United States, while generous, gives at a significantly lower percentage than many other industrialized nations. Those large and industrialized nations, together with global financial institutions, will need to continue the good work of international debt relief begun in the Jubilee year of 2000. And the developing world, in partnership with others, will need to attend to issues of accountability, transparency, and the misdirection of public resources for private gain. The Africa Monitor project of South Africa's Archbishop Ndgungane is a solid approach to those challenges. The people of the world must continue to challenge their governments to live up to this bold vision that brings together developed and developing nations to better the lives of billions of people.

The world needs the kind of leadership that can dream big dreams, challenge old and inadequate ways, and courageously seek the best for all humanity—and indeed all creation. As leaders you have a significant opportunity to build a more just and equitable world, and it will take all the gifts you have to offer—and some you may not yet recognize.

All great leadership begins in courage—the courage to dream those dreams, and to challenge unjust and corrupt systems. That courage will be repeatedly tested and tried, but it does grow stronger as it's exercised. You will discover that telling someone "no" gets easier the second and third time. You will also discover, if you haven't already, that fear usually arises out of ignorance—fear of the unknown person or idea, fear of what is untested or unexplored in yourself, and fear of the future. Most of those fears quail in the face of exploration.

Your leadership and its effectiveness will depend on your ability to see connections in unlikely places between people or ideas that haven't yet met, in the interconnected web that sustains all life on this planet and beyond, and in the reality that John Donne expressed in his poem:

No man is an island, entire of itself
every man is a piece of the continent, a part of the main
. . . any man's death diminishes me, because I am involved in mankind
and therefore never send to know for whom the bell tolls
it tolls for thee.[1]

Every single one of us is diminished by the failure of our neighbors to thrive—and so is our ability to live a full and abundant life. That is true whether the neighbor is a member of our immediate family or a woman with filariasis[2] in Namibia, a fish-slave in Ghana, or a child sold into sex-slavery in Cambodia. Their suffering limits human flourishing—yours, mine, and that of all humanity.

A deeply grounded sense of compassion, coupled with a grand and global vision, can change this world. My tradition calls that vision the reign of God, or the commonweal of God, and while your motivation may not be explicitly grounded in a religious tradition, you are here because you seek the betterment of all humanity.

It seems appropriate to say something about the religious motivation of leadership, especially in our day. Like all gifts, it is one that can be misused or used well. At its best, religious motivation leads to building up—not diminishing—all humanity and all creation. At its best, such a motivation—rooted in any of the world's great religions—seeks justice and peace and abundant life, ideally for all creatures. At its best, such a motivation seeks that vision on behalf of all, rather than some subset of humanity. Beware of religious leaders who are unwilling to serve the greater good, who insist that God loves only some, or who say that a portion of humanity is not worthy of respect or dignity. That is a hamstrung and limping version of the great dream of shalom, salaam, or *shanti* (the Sanskrit word for peace). As in the dream of Martin Luther King, Jr., we seek a world in which all children can grow and play together, unconcerned by those accidents of birth or life that others see as all-defining. We seek a world where the poor hear good news, the ill are healed and the hungry fed; where prisoners are forgiven, set free, and restored to community; where no one studies war any more. We seek a world in which the systems that maintain some in servitude or slavery are abolished, where all have the minimal right to life, liberty, and the pursuit of happiness. But even more, we seek a world where all have the right to full and abundant lives at peace with their neighbors.

Achieving a world or a community that is more whole or healthy or healed or even holy—those words all come from the same root—or more closely aligned with that great vision, will require partnerships between groups and people with similar goals but varying motivations, religious and not. The ability to sort out the godly or humane motivations from those that are less than noble is part of the challenge before us all. In some sense it is the eternal dilemma that faces all social architects. If politics is the art of the possible or the art of living in community, how can politics play an effective and fruitful role in building that just society? Jesus had a rather canny understanding of politics: in Matthew he instructed his disciples to "be wise as serpents and innocent as doves" (Matt 10:16) and in Luke (16:8) he observed that "the children of this age are more shrewd in dealing with their own generation than are the children of light." Political savvy is not a bad thing, and Jesus was clearly urging its development in service of that vision of the reign of God.

That word *savvy* is about knowing. The public service of community building requires knowledge of several kinds. Religious vision and knowledge—what is sometimes called enlightenment—can inspire people to dream dreams and think thoughts that lead them beyond narrow instinctual self-interest toward a healed world of peace and justice. That kind of knowledge may be ineffable—or hard to put into words—but it creates the passion, zeal, and energy required to struggle toward that vision. Religious or spiritual knowledge is about making meaning out of life: Why am I here? How am I meant to live? The answers usually have to do with right relationship to God, other human beings, and the rest of creation.

In this quest for knowledge, understanding the best of recent science is not a luxury; it is essential to building this vision of a healed community. Not only is the scientific method a potential arbiter of narrowly adversarial or competitive visions of reality, it is an important partner to the kind of spiritual knowing that is willing to dream beyond the mechanics of life toward equity, justice, and peace. Science is a way of understanding the workings of this world, whether at the level of quantum physics, ocean currents, and weather systems, or the dynamics of human beings in community. It is a way of knowing what we have to work with, and it can lead to testable hypotheses about the most effective means of changing what is.

The kind of political work—the living-in-community work—that you are equipping yourselves for here is a vital piece of the savvy that you will need to change this world into a place worthy of our aspirations. That savvy, however, must be joined to the whole of human possibility of which religion speaks and to the reality of this world, of which science speaks. Without the transcendent, politics can become mere manipulation; without science, politics can become blind. Together this enterprise can build a more whole, healed—and yes, holy—world for the ultimate benefit of all humanity and all creation.

Daring to Dream

Bronx, New York, USA
St. Anne's Episcopal Church
Feast of Martin Luther King, Jr.

15 January 2007

My first visit to the Bronx, which I have heard some New Yorkers define as "another culture," on the secular feast day remembering the birth of Dr. King. We celebrated a festal Eucharist together with several congregations of the Bronx. On that day we could not have imagined what would be happening two short years later, at the inauguration of Barack Obama.

Exodus 3:7–12; Psalm 77:11–20; Luke 6:27–36

Our brother Martin had a dream, born in the story of a people led out of slavery and oppression. He labored mightily to bring that dream to reality, to liberate a people still in chains and shackles a hundred years after the emancipation proclamation. You and I know that nearly forty years after his death we still have not fully achieved that dream. Some still live in oppression because of the color of their skin. Some still live in oppression because of their national origin and heritage. Some have arrived on these shores to work, but live in oppression because our system wants their labor but is not willing to allow them to become full and equal citizens.

The gospel is about the love God has for all of us. Week by week, we promise to show that love to the world by the way we live and act. Dr. King was a powerful witness to the ability of love to change the world—and for him it was the radically non-violent form of love of the gospel. It is a way of being in the world that means loving yourself and recognizing the image of God within you, and then doing the same with others. It's not rolling over and playing dead; it's not going along to get along. It is expecting the best of yourself and other people, but doing it in a way that builds up that image of God, that insists that we can all grow up into the full stature of Christ.

Non-violent loving is not necessarily easy, but it can change the world. The gospel this morning offers three concrete examples of how to love our enemies and do good to those who hate us.

Turn the other cheek. We've usually understood that to mean that we shouldn't retaliate when we're offended. But it's more. In the ancient world when a master hit a slave, or a superior struck an inferior, it was always with the back of the hand. Jesus' invitation is a subversive one. It is an "in your face" kind of response to turn the head and offer the other cheek, because it catches the offender off guard. If the offender wants to continue, it will have to be by dealing with an equal. It can't be another offhand, throwaway blow. Dr. King taught people to live in a way that says, "Even if you disregard me, I am a full human being and your equal." He taught a way of living that led to taking a seat at lunch counters and on buses. Sometimes those actions drew violent responses, from fire hoses to bullets. But those violent, disproportionate responses began to change public opinion, and to dismantle the system of domination.

If anyone takes away your coat do not withhold even your shirt. This, too, is more than it seems on the surface. It's the kind of response St. Francis of Assisi chose. If your loan is called and "the man" comes and asks for what you've offered as security, don't stop with giving your coat. Give him all your clothes, and stand there naked. In the ancient world, more than in our own, it was extremely shameful for one person to look on another person's nakedness. But it's not a tactic that is dead. In the Nigerian Delta, ongoing oil exploration and development is causing untold environmental damage and illness among the people who live there. Several years ago, after repeated attempts to negotiate with the oil companies, a large group of women marched down to the corporate offices and took off their shirts. Their action began to open the door to conversation and change.

Give to everyone who begs from you, and lend expecting nothing in return. This is probably the most challenging. Give and lend, because none of what we have is really ours—it belongs to God and we are only stewards. And don't expect a return, don't charge interest, don't ask to get it back later on. Don't give anything with strings attached, for those strings are a kind of shackle that binds the receiver and the giver. Give freely, and set the other free in turn. Generosity is disarming—whether it's giving money, or our talent and time, or risking our lives in the service of others. When Dr. King's house was bombed, he began to understand that his life was probably forfeit in the end, but he continued to love nonetheless. Two weeks ago here in New York, Wesley Autrey offered his life to save another's under a subway train—and both of them are alive today, more alive than they were before that encounter. You and I *can* keep on loving folks who disagree with us and people who hate us, and we can change the world.

Dr. King offered a life lived with that kind of freedom. His dream began in setting free the people he called Negros. But that dream continued to enlarge—to setting free those in poverty, those who suffered under systems of injustice, those who were sent to war and those who were warred upon. That is perhaps the fullest expression of loving our neighbors as ourselves—being able to see the whole world as sister or brother. That is what it means to be merciful as God is merciful. That word for mercy in Hebrew comes from the word for womb, and has a sense of care for all the children of one's womb. God is merciful in the same way a mother cares for all her children, but we affirm that God is father of us all, all of humanity and all of creation.

Nearly forty years have passed since Martin King was assassinated. Like the prophets of the Hebrew Bible, like the threat Jesus posed to the governments of his day, like the prophets of many ages since, Martin threatened the structures of oppression and domination in this country. The systems of domination in this world strike out when their poverty is revealed, when their selfishness and shame are exposed for the world to see. That stripping away of evil is the work God asks of us all. May we be tireless lovers of our enemies, ever-hopeful of seeing them in the completeness for which God created them. As long as anyone is in bondage, none of us will ever be free.

God asks us to dream dreams, love the unlovable, and have mercy on the merciless. When we do it, we join Martin in worshipping God on the mountaintop.

Mission and the Church

Raleigh, North Carolina, USA
Address to the Urban Caucus

8 February 2007

The Urban Caucus is a gathering of Episcopalians who meet regularly to strategize, learn, and support each other in working for justice in urban environments.

I'd like to begin by reflecting on the name of this body. The Urban Caucus came into existence to address mission in the city, among the people who live in the midst of our most crowded and often most impoverished communities. As I pondered your history, and the expanded sense of mission this body has developed, particularly to "be in solidarity with the poor everywhere," it occurred to me that perhaps your name should be expanded as well. Not only are the poor gathered in cities, but on the reservations where many Native Americans still live, and in the rural areas of this country, especially in Appalachia and the south. You have an enlarging sense of global mission as well, and it is not only to the city. The response of the Episcopal Church to all of God's children, however, ought to be the same—to see the suffering of human beings, made in the image of God, and to respond in ways that seek to realize God's dream of a restored and healed world.

So, I don't know if you will eventually be the Global Caucus or the Urban Caucus, but let's begin with urban, and the original mission of this body. Cities came into existence when agriculture developed to the point where people no longer had to wander around gathering or hunting their food. The settling of significant numbers of people in fixed locations was soon followed by the development of real wealth and its eventual concentration in the hands of a few. Systems of governance developed to maintain both order and that uneven division of wealth. A division of labor permitted some to devote time to leisure and pursuits of the mind while others labored on their behalf. The kind of economic division we know so well was one of the concomitant results.

Human settlement permitted the development of what we call civilization (and note the roots of that word in "citizen," that is, "one who lives in a city") and the exacerbation of human divisions. With cities and their creative nature came also the systems of oppression that have dehumanized people for millennia, and continue to do so to this day.

The poverty and human oppression that the Caucus seeks to address may have its roots in the systems of cities, but that suffering extends to all humanity and, especially in this day, to all creation. Your mission is about relieving the human suffering in this world, but also and perhaps even more importantly acting, strategizing, and advocating for change in the systems that permit and encourage that suffering. That mission is a focused understanding of what this Church claims as the mission of all the baptized: to reconcile the world to God and each other in Christ.

At the last General Convention this Church adopted a set of mission priorities to focus our common work in the three years that followed. The first priority is particularly focused on that work of reconciliation and the relief of suffering, and we have named it as the pursuit of justice and peace, framed by the Millennium Development Goals. Other priorities include work with young adults, youth, and children; reconciliation and evangelism; congregational transformation; and partnerships, both within the Anglican Communion and with ecumenical and interfaith bodies. All of them are particular ways of engaging the mission God gives us to reconcile the world. The members of the Urban Caucus will have a number of ways of engaging that mission. What might be helpful in your time together this year is to consider how the Caucus might work to expand consciousness about its mission (and its members in more local communities) and how that mission connects to our larger image of baptismal mission and ministry.

The mission of the Church might also be spoken of as building the reign of God. That vision of a healed and restored world is what you and I are charged with being and doing in this world. That dream of God reverberates throughout our long history of encounter with God—in the Hebrew Bible and in the second covenant in Jesus. Coming home again to Eden, leaving slavery in Egypt, entering the promised land, drawing all the nations to Zion, building the city of God, spreading a great banquet on the hillside and inviting everyone to take part—all these are images of a world restored to right relationship. Jesus himself acts out those images in feeding the multitudes, healing the sick and urging the people around them to feed them and restore them to community. He acts out those images in a final supper with the disciples to remind them of that great dream of God. Among his resurrection appearances are several about food and feeding people, as well as restoring communities to health and wholeness.

The closing chapters of Matthew's gospel (especially Matt 25:34–36) call us to that service of healing and reconciliation: "I was hungry and you gave me food, I was thirsty and you gave me something to drink, I was a stranger and you welcomed me, I was naked and you gave me clothing, I was sick and you cared for me, I was in prison and you visited me." The Millennium Development Goals are a contemporary illustration of the work that Jesus did himself—and of the work to which he continues to call his followers.

Some understand the mission of the Church to be primarily about the Great Commission: "Go therefore and make disciples of all nations" (Matt 28:18–19). But the mission to serve and the mission to make disciples are both ways of loving God and loving our neighbors as ourselves. One way cannot be divorced from the other. I don't believe God has any patience with arguments over whether evangelism or social justice ministry is the more important—we cannot love God and our neighbors without doing both. Evangelism must be understood through the lens of our baptismal covenant, as sharing the good news of God in Christ in both word and deed. We would do well to recall that we cannot love God whom we do not see if we do not love our neighbors whom we do see. The world is not reconciled as long as some live without—without food, good news, adequate housing, peace, clothing, or justice. The work of this Church is to build a world of *shalom*. At the risk of repeating what some of you already know well, that dream of shalom includes all those other versions of God's dream—adequate food, drink, housing, employment, health care, education, equality, and the peace that comes only when justice is present and available to all.

The Millennium Development Goals are a vision of that kind of shalom for the world. They focus on extreme poverty—the kind of poverty that prevents children from developing their mental capacity fully because their bodies and brains are malnourished, and the kind of poverty that makes people far more susceptible to disease and a shortened lifespan. The goals begin with the fact that one-third of the world's people do not have adequate caloric intake—each day, two billion people go to bed hungry. The first of the goals seeks to cut that rate in half by the year 2015—eight years from now. The other goals move on from hunger to include maternal health care, so that healthy children are brought into this world; primary education for all children, both girls and boys; gender equity and the empowerment of women. Many of these goals focus on the *anawim*, the little ones on whom Jesus' own ministry focused—widows, orphans, those with infirmities and communicable diseases, women in general, those who labored at occupations deemed unclean. Sociologists and anthropologists know that when women are educated and empowered, their families and communities quickly reap the benefits—they become healthier and develop greater capacity for life—and that's a beginning to the kind of abundant life Jesus said was our birthright. When the least among us are served, the whole community flourishes.

The Millennium Development Goals also include drastic reductions in preventable diseases such as AIDS, malaria, and tuberculosis, as well as halving childhood mortality rates. The final two goals have to do with environmentally sustainable development and the development of global partnerships, especially around debt reduction, trade, and development initiatives.

These goals seek profound, even catastrophic—in the gospel sense of over-turning—change in the way this world works (or doesn't work). But the reality is that they go only half-way. They don't reach on toward the great eschatological dreams of our faith. The first goal seeks to halve the rate of abject poverty by the year 2015. It's an achievable goal, if we're serious about doing the work involved, and it is certainly not easy work. But we can't ever sit back and say, "We've done it." Not until every human being has a full and adequate diet—not just half the starving folks in this world. Not until every child is born into this world with all the adequacy of health care for him and his mother, not until every child has a full expectation of equal education, equal rights, and equal access to the necessities and blessings of life. Not until every person has the full opportunity to use all her God-given gifts and truly know the life abundant meant for each of us.

The Millennium Development Goals (MDGs) have caught the imagination of this Church in a way that is startling. I first heard about them when the Bishop of Oregon, Bob Ladehoff, came back from Lambeth in 1998 and talked about 0.7 percent and the vision of international debt relief for a year of Jubilee. I under-stood the Jubilee concept, but that number puzzled me—where had it come from? It took years to discover that the 0.7 percent number came out of the calculations of a group of economists nearly forty years ago. They realized that if the developed nations of the world were willing to commit that small percentage of their annual income to the needs of the developing world, that global poverty could largely be eliminated.

That number has been a centerpiece of the push by Episcopalians for Global Responsibility in the growing awareness of the MDGs. The number is based on governmental giving. As a sign of solidarity, more than seventy dioceses have indicated that they, too, will give at least that percentage of their annual budgets toward international development, and will encourage congregations to do the same. There is an untold or unrecognized challenge in this story, however. The scale of funding required will not be addressed by the giving of individuals or dioceses, however generous. Giving by members of this church is an essential and prophetic act, one that challenges others (particularly those "others" called governments) to join in the work.

The MDGs can only be met by governmental generosity, and it is here that the next phase of work on the MDGs must focus. You and I, Episcopalians, and all the like-minded folk we can muster, of whatever faith or denomination, will have to lobby our government to raise the level of aid we give toward 1 percent of the annual budget. Currently the U.S. gives about a quarter of what is needed. The Scandinavian countries are the closest to that level, but it should be obvious that their economies are a good deal smaller than this one. England, France, and the other EU countries are also giving increasing portions of their budgets. Yes, our country is generous, but if we are going to build a reconciled world, we're going to have to be even more serious. If you take nothing else home from this gathering, I hope you will carry away the message that advocacy is essential. That means the willingness to lobby your senators and congressional representatives to make international development a priority. That means being willing to write letters and to call Washington to say that if children are starving in Bangladesh or dying of AIDS in Zimbabwe, that we care and we want our government to do more to put a stop to it. As Christians, we believe that the world is not supposed to permit girls to be excluded from school, or allow mothers to die in childbirth because no one will go and help. We believe that malaria is largely preventable and that all people should have clean water to drink and adequate food and shelter. We take seriously what Jesus says, that "whenever you did not do this to one of the least of these" you ignored the presence of God in your midst.

Some protest that the church is not supposed to meddle in politics. But politics is simply the art of living in community. It does not need to be a dirty word. (The Spanish language even has two words—one for politics in general and another for "dirty politics.") The kingdom of God is about a society of peace and justice, and that society will not be achieved without the willingness to use all the gifts at our disposal to realize it, including politics. All of Jesus' preaching and teaching about the kingdom of God is a pointed way of saying that God, not any human government, is in charge. Our task is to challenge those governments to live up to a higher standard.

You and I are meant to build a society of peace with justice, and we cannot do it without challenging the structures of this world, whether at the city, state, or national level. Systems of injustice do not change only through silent prayer, though prayer is essential. Taking up our crosses daily means using all the gifts we have been given—the power of prayer (silently and shouted from the housetops), the power of the vote, and the power of persuasion.

That power of prayer, political involvement, and persuasion is what the Urban Caucus is especially good and gifted at doing. You have the ability to help the rest of the church and the rest of this country realize the vision of the reign of God—in Africa and Asia, as well as in Appalachia and Appalachicola and Albany. Human communities are meant to be sustainers and empowerers of life, not sloughs of despair. You have the ability to hold out that vision of hope, and to help the citizens of this country become reconcilers and healers, rather than bearers of war and violence. It is long past time to beat our swords into plowshares, to lay down our weapons of destruction, and to build an open city of truly human relationships, rooted in the radical freedom and friendship of God.

May God bless the work, may God bless each of you, and may God bless our ability to continue to dream the dream of shalom and a creation restored.

Healing the Earth

New York, New York, USA
United Nations Consultation on the Status of Women Opening Worship Chapel of Christ the Lord

23 February 2007

A short piece preached at a service of evening prayer to welcome and open the UNCSW. Anglican women from around the globe gather each year in New York to challenge the UN to greater action on issues facing women and their children.

Lamentations 2:10–13; Psalm 131; Luke 8:40–46

Welcome. Many of you have traveled far to join this gathering of the United Nations Commission on the Status of Women. The people of this world thank you for your passion, for the healing that comes through attending to the needs of more than half of the human race. We are all grateful for your willingness to get up from your many homes and come here to work for that healing.

The readings we've heard are a tension between sitting and waiting, and getting up and doing something productive. Jeremiah's lament is about widespread suffering, children dying in the streets of starvation and disease as their lives are poured out on their mothers' breasts. He could be speaking of many parts of this world today—the ravaged villages of Darfur, the blighted American inner cities, or the poverty-stricken regions of Appalachia; he could be speaking of refugee camps in Thailand, Burundi, Kenya, or Gaza. Daily, children die from lack of food and medical care, and increasingly, girl children die where boys are more highly valued, especially in parts of India and east Asia. We know that lament of the prophet, and his words pierce our hearts as well: "What can I say to you—who can heal you?"

The psalm tells us to "wait on God." Many people throughout our history have heard that as an invitation to sit back and suffer, to say, "Who are we to try? This is far too large a task for merely human hands." In Spanish, however, the words of the psalm are a bit bolder: *Espera en Dios*. "Hope in God," or perhaps, "Expect it of God." There's a bit more movement and encouragement there.

Well, is it "Wait on God," "Expect God to do something," or is it something more active—or both? The two gospel stories of healing seem to say that the kind of waiting or expectation found in faith is absolutely essential to healing—consider how often Jesus told the sick that "your faith has made you well." But how did the daughter of Jairus and the woman with the flow of blood find their healing? The girl is healed both by the faith and expectation of her father and the bystanders, and by action. The father runs off to demand healing from Jesus, and despite the laughter of the bystanders, healing comes. The woman who's been bleeding for years is healed both by her faith and by her willingness to get up and ask for it, to put the touch on Jesus. She touches him and he responds, "Go in peace." That invitation to go in peace as a healed child of God comes to us as well. We are called to go out into the world with a vision of peace and justice, of shalom for all.

I don't think there is a single instance of healing in the gospels that doesn't involve a request or demand for it. *Help me! Make me well! Let me see!* It's the same kind of hope and expectation the psalmist talks about. It is what writer Toni Cade Bambara calls "sheer holy boldness" to demand that God respond.[3] *¡Espera en Dios!* Expect that God will answer.

When Jesus comes to Jairus's house, he says to the girl, "Get up," and then he tells the others to feed her. "Get up" is the way it's translated here, but it could also be "wake up" or "stir yourself." The same word is used to speak of raising the dead. If we want healing in this world, we have to stir ourselves to get up and demand it, and expect healing as the proper way of things. We have to touch or move people in a way that lets them feel the suffering of others. We have to believe that healing is possible and do something about it. We may even have to wake the dead in our midst—those who can't or won't feel the suffering of so many around this world—and heal them enough to get busy themselves.

You and I have a vision of what the world is supposed to look like, a vision that comes out of the depths of our tradition—the reign of God, where all have enough to eat, all illness is healed, all strife is resolved, and people live together in justice and peace. That vision of shalom is our hope, and it undergirds our faith. God's vision is stronger than death, and, indeed, after the crucifixion Jesus himself is gotten up to continue that healing work. His command to the community around the little girl is the same one we get: Now, get up—you've been healed. Come to the table and eat. But it's not just a call to those of us gathered here today. It's a call to the whole world: Get up! Expect and demand the kind of healing God envisions for us all! Go and feed the world!

I met a woman last fall who touched me and many others with her story. Somaly Mam was sold into sex slavery as a young girl. When she finally emerged from her chains and found some healing herself, she went back into those dungeons and brought other girls out of their bondage. She bought them, redeemed them for life, and took them to a refuge where they might begin to heal. She continues that work today, one girl at a time.

I met another woman last fall who equips women in Afghani villages to better themselves and their families. Connie Duckworth, through an enterprise called Arzu, has helped women weavers to improve their product, and pays them 150 percent of the going rate for their rugs—but only if they agree to send their daughters to school.

I know a woman in this country who fifteen years ago looked at her community, a place depressed by the failure of all its traditional industries. She could see that while women needed to go back to work and to school, they had no childcare. She went to her church and said, "I want to use our Sunday school rooms to start a daycare. It will work if I can find seven children." Today that daycare is the center of community life, the third-largest employer in the county, and a source of hope and healing to women and men, girls and boys of all ages.

You can probably tell stories like these from your own experience. One person *can* change this world, in small ways that can lead to incredible healing. Together women can lead this world into the vision God has for us all. Bless your labors, that there may come a time when children do not die in their mothers' arms, when girls everywhere live in freedom and equality, without fear of violence or oppression. May God's reign be known on earth.

Swords into Ploughshares

New York, New York, USA
Recognition of the UN Communion Office
and the UN Observer
Evening Prayer
Chapel of Christ the Lord

11 September 2007

A service to celebrate the work of the Anglican Communion Observer at the United Nations, and its newest occupant, Hellen Wangusa.

Micah 4:1–5; Magnificat; Matthew 5:43–48

Welcome to all of you—those associated with the United Nations, with the Anglican Observer's office, or with the Episcopal Church center. It is a delight to welcome you to this space, and to gather to give thanks for the work of the UN Observer, the gifts Hellen Wangusa brings to that post, and the gifts others on her staff bring to their work.

The United Nations claims that its purpose is "to bring all nations of the world together to work for peace and development, based on the principles of justice, human dignity and the well-being of all people."

The scripture readings we have just heard echo but also underlie that understanding, particularly through the image of a city set on a hill, where God is worshiped, and to which all the nations come seeking justice. Those images first spoke of Jerusalem as the city of peace, and despite the continuing struggle over that particular city, the Abrahamic faiths still hold up that dream of a city that is a source of justice for all.

The United Nations, in the minds of many, is also an image of that city of God, in which all the nations may find peace. When the nations gather, seeking peace, we still dream that justice will prevail. When human beings begin to converse together, to seek understanding and cooperation—even in multiple languages and with many interpreters—that possibility begins. We claim a heritage, common to the Abrahamic faiths, that God's justice will eventually triumph, and that justice has something to do with an ideal city—an interconnected and interdependent human community.

The mission of the United Nations is peace with justice, the same mission that is claimed here in Micah and in the psalm for Jerusalem, the city built on a hill. Each and every one who labors in that city to build a just and peaceful world participates in God's dream. Ambassadors, translators, mail clerks, and those who maintain the building in which the nations gather—all contribute to that vision of possibility.

We live woefully short of that vision, that dream of righteousness and justice, especially when Jerusalem, the city that is the model for that vision, continues to be fractured and divided, when it produces more strife than peace, when plowshares continue to be reforged into swords and weapons of war.

We're here tonight to recognize and celebrate the ministry of one particular office, which exists to advise and challenge and inform both the members of the UN and the members of the Anglican Communion. The Office of the Anglican Observer seeks opportunities to sue for peace. This office has a prophetic role, and like the great prophets of the Hebrew scriptures, that role has two essential parts.

Prophets cry woe to those who subvert and violate the dream of peace with justice, and they also cry encouragement and hope to those who yearn for a better world. Every time Hellen Wangusa shares the statistics of poverty, disease, and conflict with those who labor at the UN, she is doing the first kind of prophetic work. Every time she listens to a story of woe and offers hope and possibility, she is doing the second kind.

Prophets lurk on the margins, for they need the perspective that comes with seeing and hearing those outside the city of dreams, those who do not yet enjoy its peace. Prophets also need the perspective to see into a community of insiders who believe they already live in that city of dreams.

Prophets are not always popular. An American social commentator and preacher named Garrison Keillor puts it bluntly: Prophets are not much fun to have around, he points out, and they don't get invited to a lot of birthday parties. Prophets often experience pain and isolation in their work, and as Jesus notes, the prophets most often die in Jerusalem. Prophets produce the strongest reaction in the place that should most welcome their voice—the dream of peace often evokes massive and violent resistance. Most governments are not eager to hear the voice of prophets—in either of their roles. Prophets need and deserve their own communities of support, and I hope and pray that is why you are here tonight.

We are also remembering the violence wrought in this city six years ago. The sources of that violence have something to do with the dreams that others have associated with this city and this nation, dreams of greed and acquisitiveness, unholy dreams that don't have much to do with peace and justice. The prophetic work that continues in the aftermath of the violence of 9/11 is to seek peace, and dream of a world in which people of all faith traditions and all nations can live together in justice.

That dream has a great deal to do with the work of the United Nations. Those who continue to dream of nations living together in peace challenge the deadly destruction that was wrought here in 2001, and is wrought daily around the globe. Peace-making is dangerous and difficult work. But it is the work that is most worth doing.

Peacemakers bring remarkable gifts to their work, beginning with the ability to dream of a city where justice for all is both law and normal expectation. Peacemakers teach others how to see beyond division, how to notice the fundamental humanity that unites us all. Here in the church we call that fundamental unity "being made in the image of God." We insist that each life is of ultimate value and dignity. The UN Observer shares the vocation of visionary: she is always on the lookout to see the things that unite us. The Observer and her staff also share the vocation of prophetic challenger: they are always on the lookout to see dignity and worth even in those who hate us. We, too, begin to make peace when we can see that our mortal enemy is made in the image of God.

There is a remarkable story of a man imprisoned in Asia during the Second World War, who was asked how he survived the brutality of his captors and how he was able eventually to forgive them: "I imagined the most vicious of them as a babe held in his mother's arms," he replied, "and I kept that image before me, day after day. It made it impossible to hate."

We have special reason to remember perpetrators of violence as babes held in their mothers' arms this night. The UN Observer also has the challenge of reminding us of all the children of God whose lot is violence. She and her staff call us to remember hungry children, all who suffer from disease, women who never know basic human dignity, indigenous peoples who are ignored, devalued, and exploited, and this abused earth which is our only home. The Observer's work tells us where there is no peace, and challenges us to go forth and make peace.

Together, we can dream of *Yerushalayim*—Jerusalem—city of dreams. Together, we can challenge the cities and nations of this world to beat their swords into hoes and shovels, and turn their cannons and grenade launchers into fertilizer spreaders. We can dream and work for a world where no one learns war any more, where every human being enjoys the abundance of vine and orchard, where every person on the planet has not just enough to stave off hunger, but enough to feast and celebrate.

Sown in the Heart of Christ

San Antonio, Texas, USA
Trinity University
EYE opening
8 July 2008

The Episcopal Youth Event is an every-three year gathering of high school students from all over the Episcopal Church. More than nine hundred young people and four hundred adults attended this opening presentation.

Have you ever planted a garden or done some farming? Do you remember a Sunday school project where you planted some seeds in a paper cup? Did all of the little plants come up looking identical?

The seeds we plant don't always come up the way we expect. Sometimes the flowers that come from a bunch of seeds are different colors, or there's one white one while all the rest are red. Even genetically cloned seeds have some variation, and a lot depends on the rain and the soil and the sunshine.

How are you coming up? What are your flowers looking like? What about the fruit or seed you're going to produce? How's the world going to be different because you've been here?

It's not just the DNA your parents gave you, or the environment you're growing up in—like where you live or the kind of parents you have or how tough a school you go to. You have something vital—something life-giving—to offer the seed planted in you.

When you were baptized Jesus planted in you the promise that you are loved beyond knowing. That word, "promise," means literally "a sending forth." It's a hope—and more than a hope. Like God's word, it intends to do what it promises—that what is given you will bear fruit.

When you were baptized, God said the same thing to you that he said to Jesus at his baptism: "You are my beloved, and in you I am well pleased." That's a promise that God will keep on loving you even if you turn out to be a red flower instead of a white one. God will keep on loving you even if you spend a lot of time looking pretty wilted. God will keep on loving you even if you don't produce any fruit. God hopes for fruit, but God's love doesn't depend on it. God's love is something like the sunshine that lets the plant grow. We don't see the sun all the time, but the plant is getting ready to grow even when it's dark—when it's a seed that hasn't emerged from the soil, and during the hours of night when the sunflower turns its face to catch the first rays of a rising sun.

You've been sown in the heart of Christ, planted in abiding love, and that promised and promising love means you are loved beyond imagining. God intends the best for you, even when what you experience around you falls short of that promise.

Your job is to live into that promise, remember that you were planted with hope, and let that promise issue forth, be sent out, to bless everyone and everything around you. More life is possible, abundant life is meant for us all, and you have a part to play.

You have something to do with the place the seed has landed. Will you be a rocky path, dry and shallow dirt, or fertile soil? Will you cultivate good soil, and produce thirty or sixty or a hundred times as much as that seed of promise?

Part of my work takes me all over the Church. I get to wander around the Church, see the seeds growing and the harvest being gathered. I get to observe, and encourage—like talking to the plants—but I don't do the harvesting. The harvest isn't finished until the end of time. God's abiding love keeps hoping for more.

What kinds of fruitfulness do I see?

Episcopal Community Services in San Diego is a ministry that offers transition housing for the homeless mentally ill. Another of their ministries offers after-school tutoring for Sudanese and Burmese immigrant children and young people. I got to meet bright and disciplined young people who are eager to give back the love that's been showered on them, even though they can tell you horror stories about life and human cruelty.

St. Patrick's in Geumgan, South Korea, runs a day center for "abandoned" mentally disabled kids and adults. They do it in one small room in an office building. They serve twenty of the mentally disabled in their town, but there are another ninety people in town not being served. They're trying to raise money for a bigger building so they can serve more people, and serve more effectively.

Sometimes the fruitfulness is literally about gardens—community gardens in Dallas, Texas, and Eagle Butte, South Dakota, that are planted and tended to feed the hungry. In Dallas it's about feeding homeless people and folks trying to get by on inadequate income. On the Sioux reservation in South Dakota, it's about fighting the grinding poverty and the total unavailability of decent food within dozens of miles. There are no grocery stores, and you know what gas costs right now.

People have to decide if they're going to feed their children what's available at the convenience store, or drive to town. Hardly a question when you're going to spend all your money on gas just to go one way. Every community in this Church is being affected by rising food prices and the cost of fuel to deliver it, whether it's to your family, the local food bank, or Meals on Wheels for seniors who can't leave home.

Bear abundant fruit, Jesus says.

For decades, we thought that the green revolution was going to help us feed the world. Episcopal Relief and Development and others are teaching better farming methods, and sharing seed that's better suited to different climates, and it is making a difference. But in order to have a bountiful harvest, to feed the world, we also need to work for change.

Dom Helder Camara is famous for saying, "When I give food to the poor they call me a saint; when I ask why the poor have no food, they call me a communist."

Helder Camara was the Roman Catholic archbishop in northeastern Brazil from 1964 to1985. He died in 1999 at the age of ninety. Many people called him "a mystic in love with the poor." He was the first to talk about the spiral of violence, a phrase you will hear frequently these days.

He pointed out that most violence is the result of truly awful poverty and three kinds of responses to that poverty. That spiral of violence starts with the injustice that keeps so many people poor and on the outside of society, like the supposedly banned caste system in India, that still says only certain kinds of people do the really dirty work, and the racism here that still suggests that some are less worthy than others. You have heard some say, "We don't need *those* people.'" Well, Jesus is one of *those* people, and that is a great part of what it means for God to walk among us in human flesh. The injustice of that kind of wretched poverty often comes with the assumption that this is "just the way things are" and you will hear people quote Jesus saying, "The poor you will always have with you." That's not what he meant. He did mean that as long as we live in hopelessness, we will never figure out how to change that poverty.

The second part of violence is the physically violent response by people who endure that poverty year after year and generation after generation—like the violence in Gaza, or the riots in China after the big earthquake, or race riots here in the United States, or the food riots in Haiti.

And the third aspect is what happens in response to those violent outbursts. Governments and those "in charge" come along and put down those riots—violence is repressed with violence. You can see it happening in Israel's response to the violence being exported from Gaza in the form of rockets. You can see it in Myanmar, where the generals are putting down demonstrations. You can see it here when Immigration and Customs Enforcement puts most of its energy into punishing the weakest, rather than those who hire them.

Helder Camara's response, like Jesus', is to say that the only moral response to all these kinds of violence is the use of love—non-violence—in seeking justice. It has to begin at the first level, by acting in ways to end injustice. And Camara insists that it is those who feel injustice routinely—and the young—who are the ones with the energy to motivate change.

He was writing at the time of Vietnam. You have grown up through the wars in Afghanistan and Iraq, and you know something of the beginnings of work toward justice in the Millennium Development Goals. This is your vocation. This is what love in action looks like—putting an end to structural violence and "disposable people." There are no disposable people, only God's beloveds. You know that, because that promise has been planted in you. Spreading and sharing that sense of being beloved is an essential part of bearing abundant fruit, thirtyfold, sixtyfold, and a hundredfold.

What is your harvest going to look like?

Christ in the Stranger

San Diego, California, USA
St. James by the Sea

6 April 2008

This was preached at the close of a diocesan visit to San Diego, in a wealthy, urban congregation that has a very good education program on current social issues, for its members and the wider community.

Acts 2:14a, 36–47; Psalm 116; 1 Peter 1:17–23; Luke 24:13–35

I was in the Holy Land during this last Holy Week. When we were there by chance we met Cindy and Craig Corrie, whose daughter Rachel was killed by a bulldozer in Gaza five years ago. She was protesting the Israeli government's destruction of a Palestinian home. We heard over and over from Palestinian Christians about forced evictions and houses being demolished. The West Bank is occupied territory, controlled by Israel, and building permits are very difficult for Palestinians to obtain. Tens of thousands of permits have gone to Israeli settlers in the last few years, but fewer than a hundred to Palestinians. The usual response is to go ahead and build anyway, without a permit, when your family outgrows its quarters or a son or daughter marries and you need another room.

The people in Gaza—both Christians and Muslims—live in refugee camps, and Israel builds settlements for Jews in the West Bank, both Israelis and foreign immigrants. My image of both those realities had been of tent cities, but the reality on the ground is of cement apartment blocks, most of them surrounded by barbed wire and other defenses. Both experiences are a long way from settled and peaceful domestic life—the kind of life that the prophets hold up as *shalom*, living in peace and justice with neighbors you respect because they are made in the image of God. That vision assumes that all are neighbors, and that there are no longer any strangers.

When Jesus walks up alongside those two disciples going to Emmaus, they ask him if he's the only stranger in Jerusalem who doesn't know what's going on. The word for stranger that's used there, *paroikos*, actually means a resident alien, literally someone who lives outside or alongside a normal house, *oikos*. The writer of the first letter of Peter uses the same word when he instructs his readers to "live in reverent fear in the time of your exile." The exiled one, the alien or stranger, is a long way from living in peace at home.

So who is the stranger? The disciples call Jesus the alien, but Peter's letter says it is we who are the aliens. The writer of the letter to the Ephesians (2:19) says that we are no longer strangers and aliens, but citizens with the saints and members of the household of God—that same vision of a world where all God's children live together in peace. The early church uses the word *paroikia* as a description of the faith community who lives like that—as aliens in the world. It's the root of our word, "parish." Ever thought of your fellow parishioners as aliens—maybe after a difficult vestry meeting?

We are the aliens, the ones living outside God's dream, outside the heavenly city. We are the ones waiting outside the gate, working to build a new city where all can be citizens of the household of God. In some real sense, none of us gets to be a citizen there until we all are. We are all living in temporary quarters.

That sense of being alien is not one most of us find terribly comfortable. Lots of Americans point their fingers at others whom they call aliens, usually with the adjective "illegal." Luke's Emmaus story is about a whole crew of illegal folk—Jesus, who is executed as a criminal outside the city gates, and his followers who don't have the legal standing to make themselves known in a culture that doesn't recognize their legitimacy. And that is a really big deal at the time Luke puts his gospel down on paper—Rome has just destroyed the Temple because of all the subversive activity going on in Jerusalem. Nobody's safe—neither the Jews who call themselves Pharisees nor the ones who call themselves followers of Jesus' way. They are all aliens in their own land.

As global citizens in the twenty-first century, we're beginning to realize that none of us lives in a permanent and unchanging home, either, and that the way we treat our quarters—our *oikos*—has a big impact on all the other residents of this squatter's camp. Our ecology and our economy—both have their roots in that same word for house—are dependent on how we live in this temporary house, this parish we call earth.

Yet the further point of Jesus' encounter on the road—and there is something important there about being on a journey—comes when the three travelers settle down for an evening meal. When we share food, we get a taste of home. It's as simple and as profound as that. Coffee hour *is* as important as worship, for it's another reminder of the temporary quarters we share, and the reality that we know God's presence when we can lower our defenses and share the stuff of life.

What drives people to insist on the permanence of their claims to land has a lot to do with fear. Fear that there won't be enough—enough space, enough safety, enough food. Yet God comes to us whether we are ready or not—as a stranger and an alien—in the homely act of breaking bread.

In my short time in the diocese of San Diego, I've seen lots of examples of how this part of the Church is working to give aliens a home—the resettled refugees from Sudan and now Burma who are being tutored after school; the homeless mentally ill who are getting help to stabilize their lives and their living arrangements; the children of immigrants who are learning social skills and nutrition along with the alphabet and numbers, skills they will need to grow up and be full members of this community. Your own ministry here at St. James is about walking with people on their spiritual journeys. That tells me you already know, at a deep level, that none of us is really yet at home. I was intrigued to see the announcement for a talk this coming Wednesday on migration from Oaxaca to the United States, another way to learn about being on the road together.

Being on the road is what the early Christians called their community—"the way" or "the road." They didn't come to be called Christians for quite a while. They knew themselves to be aliens, wanderers like Jesus, and like him, they had no place to lay their heads.

The reality of resurrection sometimes comes to us in strange guises, and sometimes it even comes to us as we meet strangers. Most often it has something to do with hospitality—eating together, helping another to find a more stable home, building a community that says we can serve each other even if we're still ultimately homeless.

The day after Easter the bishop of Jerusalem went to Jordan to meet with King Abdullah, who is Muslim. The two of them were on very good terms, and there were growing Anglican congregations in Jordan. Bishop Suheil went to talk about the diocesan institutions in Jordan, particularly the schools that serve both Muslim and Christian children. On Thursday of that week, he went back to Jordan to preside at the dedication of land that the king has given to the Anglican diocese. The bishop dedicated that land on the banks of the Jordan River, at the traditional site of Jesus' baptism, and plans to build a church and a guest house there that will welcome all strangers. Those strangers can expect to meet Jesus in their midst.

The next time we meet an alien, will we recognize Jesus in our midst?

A Hundredfold

Salisbury, England
Salisbury Cathedral

13 July 2008

I visited Salisbury Diocese, and was hosted by the dean for several days before the Lambeth Conference. The bishops of Sudan were also visiting the diocese at the same time. On 12 July, we walked in pilgrimage from the site of the old cathedral, several miles into town, ending at the 750-year-old "new" cathedral. The Sudanese were the fastest walkers!

Romans 8:1–11; Matthew 13:1–9; 18–23

I bring you greetings from Episcopalians in Taiwan, Micronesia, Honduras, Colombia, Ecuador, Venezuela, Haiti, Dominican Republic, Puerto Rico, the British and U.S. Virgin Islands, a group of churches in six countries of Europe, and the one hundred dioceses in the United States. They remember you in their prayers, and I ask yours for them.

Yesterday on our pilgrimage from Old Sarum to this new cathedral all the walkers got to see something of your countryside. There are rich and fertile fields filled with nearly ripe crops, and hedgerows with a riotous variety of flowers, bushes, and trees. That abundance is the result of seeds spread by birds and small animals, by the wind, and by farmers. At this season, most of that sowing seems well on its way to bearing abundant fruit.

But not every part of the world lets seeds grow quite so easily. In the desert, or in the mountains above tree line, very few plants manage to prosper. Most of the seeds that fall never even germinate, let alone produce fruit or seed. It's a rare sight to see a plant above ten thousand feet—at that altitude, to begin to germinate the seed has to have the luck to fall in a crevice or protected place where there is enough moisture. It's still unlikely it will ever establish a root system and find enough organic and mineral soil to grow. There's a small example on the west face of this building, up above the doors, where there is a little plant established on the stone.

There are some other odd places that seem surprisingly fertile. My office is in the center of New York City, and I can look out and see potted plants and trees on rooftops and balconies, many stories above the ground. People plant lovely things in those containers. Some of them are well-tended, and some are abandoned after a season. But everywhere there is dirt, things grow—grass, weeds, the odd flower. The seeds come on the wind or from birds, and they take root in all sorts of strange places. And then there are the very strange things that people plant along the street. I've seen mature banana plants growing along a sidewalk in a climate where they will never survive past October. No fruit will ever be harvested. Why did somebody bother?

That doesn't seem to be a question that bothers God. Jesus is more interested in reminding his hearers that God's grace and favor is broadcast with far greater abandon than the birds or the banana-planter. The sower scatters seed without counting the cost. And that produces a real tension for many of us. It feels wasteful to throw away seeds that have no chance of doing anything productive.

God's economy is often a challenge to us. Perhaps that profligacy makes more sense when we recognize that a seed that *does* take root can produce thirty- and sixty- and a hundredfold. That is something to celebrate.

Yesterday we dedicated a statue on the West Front of this cathedral, depicting Canon Ezra, a martyr of Sudan. He was a priest of the Moro tribe, who translated the Bible into his people's language. He was killed in a crossfire during the civil war, on Good Friday 1991. But his witness continues to bear abundant fruit.

Think for a moment about the long line of planted seeds that has led to that fruit. Jesus' disciples spread the word in and around their communities. Thomas is reputed to have gone east as far as India. Paul was one of the first to move around the Mediterranean. Philip the Ethiopian eunuch reportedly went back to his native land. Within a relatively few decades, Roman soldiers knew the good news and spread it among their cohorts. And they came to Britain. When Augustine arrived here several centuries later, he found the seeds had already begun to bear fruit, although some of it was strange to his taste. The word continued to spread from here—even into enemy territory. Celtic monks moved even farther afield. Sometimes, maybe even often, the seed did fall on dry and rocky ground. But the sowers continued to spread the word. Centuries went by. New sowers went out with merchants and adventurers around the globe. And less than a hundred years ago—just yesterday in the history of this place—sowers went to Sudan. And the word grew deep roots in that place, and flourished. The Sudanese bishops tell me that the recent missionaries found evidence of the work that Philip had done, just as Augustine did here.

The recent mission work in Sudan could have come only after the church here in England learned something new about God's profligacy. When much of the world practiced human slavery, including Britain and the United States, it was considered wasteful at the very least to bother planting God's word in Africa. That work required learning a deeper truth about God's grace and favor—that it is meant for all human beings. It required Christians in the northern hemisphere to re-learn that there is no division in God—that in Christ there is no longer Jew nor Greek, slave nor free, male nor female. No division based on ethnicity, race, or gender. That seed took a very long time to bear fruit. Some of it is still struggling to take root.

But the fact that it did had a great deal to do with the single-mindedness of people like William Wilberforce, who spent his life working to end the slave trade. His political skill, and the passion of abolitionist preachers, in a society deeply conflicted about the stature of human beings darker than themselves, finally shifted the legal status of slavery here. It took another sixty years to formally end— Zanzibar was the last place from which slaves were traded, and it was the British navy that eventually convinced the ruler there to swear off slaving in 1895.

The seeds of the gospel eventually made their way to Sudan, and quickly sprang up. The witness of many like Canon Ezra shows evidence of deep soil and a fruitful harvest. Yet the links this diocese has had with Sudan over thirty-five years have brought seed back here as well, seed that is beginning to take root in new ways, here in a place where it has grown for nearly two millennia. Those seeds continue to invite this diocese into far deeper understandings of what it means to be sisters and brothers in Christ.

God continues to do a new thing, even in unexpected places.

God's grace and favor still falls on people some societies find inappropriate. Why plant bananas, indeed. Many even supposedly Christian nations find it difficult to treat immigrants as worthy recipients of full Christian welcome and hospitality. We often have the same attitudes toward gay people. At times we've treated the mentally disabled with equal disdain. Wars can only start when we decide that the enemy has no possible value in God's economy. That limited view of appropriate seed-beds for God's love knows no national bounds. We see evidence of tribal understandings all over the world, whenever we see people insisting that only this kind of soil can bear good fruit, but not that over there—it's too rocky, or the climate is completely wrong—or why bother? But there are no tribes in Christ. There is no one who can be considered beyond the reach of God's loving sowing.

Loosening the soil so that it might be fertile terrain has a great deal to do with softening our own hearts. When we're certain that a person can't possibly be a God-bearer, it is our own soil that fills with rocks, or grows massive thorns. This is a particularly religious, and Christian, challenge, for we search endlessly to be certain that we are doing it right. But when we get too certain about God and God's judgment, our soil starts to crust over. Then it's time to let ourselves be tilled, to allow our soil to be turned over by the surprising love of the gospel and the unexpected nature of divine economics. Indeed, some of that riotous abundance out there doesn't even depend on seeds for growth—consider potatoes, for example, or onions. God's seed planting can happen without what look to us like seeds.

Who are the banana plants for you—the impossible seedbeds for God's word of hyper-abundant love? That is our opportunity to bear fruit—thirtyfold, sixty-fold, and a hundredfold. Have a blessed plowing season.

PART TWO

PROPHETS AND PEACEMAKERS

The Church as Prophetic Witness

Boksburg, South Africa
Towards Effective Anglican Mission,
an International Conference on Prophetic Witness,
Social Development and HIV and AIDS

14 March 2007

The TEAM Conference was an all-Anglican gathering to challenge the Communion to be more effective partners in meeting the Millennium Development Goals. This was the last major address of the gathering.

What is a prophet? The word means one who speaks for God—someone who, like Isaiah or Jeremiah, dares to critique the evils of human systems and to speak a vision for what God believes things should look like. A prophet is a person who imagines—and articulates—the godly characteristics to which a human society could and should aspire.

The great prophets of the Hebrew scriptures routinely offered a different perspective of what Israel and her governors should be paying attention to, especially feeding the poor and caring for orphans and widows and aliens. And the reason for doing so, repeated over and over again, is "because you were slaves in Egypt." Out of that horribly dehumanizing experience in Egypt, the Jews received a particular vocation to remember and respond to others in like circumstances. The prophets remind Israel that all humanity is kin under the skin. Israel may be a chosen people, but that choosing is for the greater life of others. At a very important level, it is only the small details of history that have led some to the promised land and others into radical poverty. The great prophetic universality that emerges in Isaiah proclaims that Israel exists for the world—and as Christians we share that understanding.

Our tradition has a rich heritage of prophets, both in and beyond the Bible. Jesus speaks of himself as Wisdom's prophet in the gospels, and his deeds and words can perhaps be most creatively understood in a prophetic framework.

His choice of companions, the images he uses in parables, his cursing of fig trees and turning of tables—all of these are ways of speaking for God about the dismal state of the world and the creative possibilities of God's dreams. Even the scandals we call the incarnation and the resurrection make more sense in a prophetic framework—maybe not in the world's linear, cause-and-effect terms, but as God's response to those who "cry in the wilderness." That pattern of divine attention to cries in the wilderness underlies all of what we call salvation history—and it's important to recognize that it's not over and done with at the last page of Revelation. God continues to lure us into a world that looks more like eternity, more like a heavenly banquet, more like God is Lord and not we ourselves.

God's vision for this created world has a great deal to do with the aims of the Millennium Development Goals—with relieving hunger, providing education, caring for the sick, working for the full and equal dignity of all human beings, and caring for all creation. As people of faith, we affirm that we are involved with the lives of others, whether they live next door or across the world, whether they are Christian or Anglican or not, and even whether they are currently living or not. When we say we believe in the communion of the saints, it includes those who have come before us, but it must also include those yet to breathe this air of earth. We are caretakers and caregivers of all of God's creation, both present and yet to come—that is an important Christian recognition of the eschatological implications of the MDGs.

The MDGs begin with a prophetic naming of the ways God's children suffer—the billion people who go to bed hungry each night, the children who die needlessly when preventable disease takes their lives, the women who die in childbirth, and the children who don't receive the care that ensures a healthy beginning and the real possibility of abundant life. The MDGs hint at the kind of vision prophets have always held out—a world where all have not only enough to eat, but abundance enough for feasting, where all children can expect to live out the full years of their lives in health, where no one is oppressed because of gender or disease or disability, where all can enjoy the abundance of orchard and vineyard.

But the MDGs only begin to address that kind of eschatological vision. The first goal seeks only to halve the kind of desperate poverty that keeps people starving. It does not reach beyond to that vision of a heavenly banquet. The goals are a great start, but it will take the vision of faith—a vision rooted in God's intent for all creation—to keep us moving toward that kind of radically abundant life for the whole world.

The prophets God has continually sent us have an ability to speak clearly about what is and what could be. They include the great Hebrew saints who argue for justice in the gate and offer a vision of the possible, as well as those who have come since the canon of scripture was closed. Francis of Assisi spoke about all creation, and even the death that comes to us all, as sister and brother. Francis's actions spoke even more loudly about the Christian vocation to care for the hungry and ill. His own diminishment in worldly terms became his increase, and the increase of the poor for whom he labored.

We have a uniquely Anglican tradition of prophets as well—from Elizabeth I, Richard Hooker, and Hilda of Whitby, who spoke for unity in diversity, to George Herbert and Julian of Norwich, who shared with us their awareness of the movement of the spirit in the everyday and little things of life. Some of the great prophets of our tradition were involved in major critique and change of socially accepted norms. William Wilberforce campaigned tirelessly for an end to the slave trade, as did David Livingstone and Bishop Steere in Zanzibar. In spite of support for the status quo from many parts of Christian and Anglican tradition, all of those prophets challenged the spiritual wisdom of their day. Those who worked to abolish slavery went head-to-head with a received wisdom that most often said slaves should obey their masters. But the prophetic response of abolitionists offered a larger and more abundant vision that insisted that all human beings are made in the image of God and deserve full and equal dignity.

That tradition of prophecy has continued through the generations within Anglicanism. Consider the work of Archbishop Temple, who said this church is the only institution that exists primarily for the good of those outside it. Consider the life of Desmond Tutu, who challenged apartheid and, when that system finally broke, sought to heal it through affirming the place of both offender and offended in the same body of Christ. The tradition of prophecy is not dead; indeed it rings through our work here in South Africa and all around the world.

That prophetic tradition insists that full and abundant life is meant for all God's creatures, not just those who happen to live in prosperous communities or countries. There is a strand of Christian tradition, not unknown in Anglicanism, that says that prosperity is a blessing born out of righteousness, but the prophetic tradition always speaks against that kind of self-righteousness. The prophetic tradition insists that each one of us is responsible for the flourishing of our brothers and sisters, wherever and however they now struggle to live. This prophetic tradition challenges all of us to speak truth to power, to say to our governments and to the world that there is something gravely wrong with a world where the division between rich and poor continues to expand, where some live in palaces and recline on ivory couches while others starve outside the gates. This tradition also gives us a vision for what is possible, and our brothers and sisters at the United Nations have offered a framework for how we might partner in response.

The Millennium Development Goals are a start, a beginning to that great eschatological vision we have received—where all are not only fed, but invited to a banquet, where no one dies of disease or infirmity before the expected end to life. It is a world where the resources of all are shared, available so that each might flourish and enjoy that vision of abundant life. But the MDGs are only a start. They are a concrete vision of progress toward that vision, and they are achievable, if we have the will.

And that will and willingness is the root of the challenge. To move forward effectively, we must engage the attitudes that say it's not possible, will cost too much, is unrealistic, or is simply the fantastic and futile dream of fools. The faith within us is the starting point of our response. The prophets tell us that sometimes our vocation is to play the holy fool, to dream impossible dreams, and to hope in ways that make no human sense.

The history of God's prophetic action in ages past is what we have to carry into this inspired work. If we can say that God came among us in human form, and that all human beings are made in that divine image, then ignoring or repudiating that image in people across the world is an opting out of abundant life. Some might say it is choosing hell. If God has done such ridiculous things in the past, who are we to argue?

We have this hope planted within us, and we have the resources to make this dream possible. The resources are diverse—the vision itself, our communities of faith and the networks they represent, financial and personnel resources, and the will and ability to advocate in the systems that perpetuate injustice.

The communities of faith we represent are one of the largest on-the-ground delivery systems for human well-being in the world. Where else but in our churches do people come together week by week to seek health and salvation? And it is essential to remember that salvation means the health and full flourishing of the whole human person—it is not only a supposed spiritual portion of ourselves that is healed in relation to God, but our whole being. If incarnation means nothing else, it means that God took the human condition seriously enough to join it, in all its complexity and organic messiness. Salvation is for all humanity and it is for the whole person, however much we might like to divide that being up into parts we label physical, moral, psychological, sexual, intellectual, or spiritual. God is *for* all of us—the whole person and all humankind. If our communities of faith are not involved in that wholeness of salvation, they're missing something. The good news is that increasing numbers of faith communities in our tradition do understand this mind-body-spirit wholeness, and the interconnectedness of the whole body of Christ and the whole body of God's creation. When some are starving in Sudan, the entire body is injured. We are beginning to recognize that other parts of the body can feel the hunger of those who are suffering.

The networks represented here are without equal in this world; they are the most remarkable nexus of possibility for delivering abundant life. We have the delivery system on the ground already that can feed people, encourage education, provide vaccinations and disease prevention, organize people to address water needs, and partner with others. Our churches are not unlike the ancient tribes of Israel, ready to be networked for the good of the whole people of God. If we understand our mission as transformation of this world, then we must use every resource available to accomplish that mission.

The opportunity that is the Anglican Communion is a gift given for a reason, to bring healing to all. Our salvation is wrapped up in the healing of others. We have opportunities to serve this vision of wholeness, through the network of our communion, with Anglicans, Lutherans, and other committed partners. We've had that vision planted within us, and we've been given the voice and the will to collaborate to see this vision advanced. It will take the best that is within us as the spirit continues to move us onward—even when it feels like we're wandering in the wilderness. But it is a journey that we cannot avoid if we intend to be faithful.

Among our many resources are our governments. Our voices, raised on behalf of the widows and orphans and the aliens in our midst, can motivate governments to respond and participate in this vision of healing the world. Like the prophets of ancient Israel, we have been called to proclaim justice in the gate, to rise up and insist that the hungry be fed, the naked clothed, and the suffering provided relief. We know that is God's will for all creation. The MDGs offer real possibility for bringing that vision about.

We live in the first era of human history when it is truly possible to provide the basic stuff of life for all humanity. We have the resources, but they are not distributed in a way that makes this easy work. We also have all the ancient human resistance to sharing those resources—human greed, the lust for power, the desire to be God. Our faith has much to say about all kinds of resistance to loving God and loving our neighbors as ourselves.

We also have a growing awareness of the challenges of providing relief and development funds and building partnerships in ways that are most effective. We must take seriously the gifts already present in developing nations, and partner in ways that are respectful of the dignity of all persons, while holding them accountable—that is a prophetic task as well.

Prophetic work is about holding the body accountable for how it treats all of its members—the poor, the strangers, women as well as men, *and* the rich and powerful who often control government and political systems. Each of us is responsible for the other, and none of us can be healed or saved unless all are. That insight about communities of salvation is a principle central to our Hebraic roots. It has too often been forgotten in the developed world, even in Christendom. None is expendable—not slave, not woman, not child, not the lame or halt or blind. All show us the image of God, and if we do not respond to the suffering Christ in those least, we are ignoring God in our midst. As we have done (or not done) to the least of these, we have done to Jesus, or we have ignored him. We live in a world increasingly connected by mass communication. We know far more about suffering around the world than we did even a generation ago. That makes it even more incumbent on us to respond, and the task of Anglicans and all people of faith is to hold ourselves and the whole world accountable for that suffering.

The good news is that we have a growing capacity to respond to that suffering in a global way. The AIDS pandemic is a remarkable example. Fully 40 percent of the money spent on responding to AIDS and HIV infection goes through communities and institutions of faith. And it is safe to say that much of the rest of the response is urged by people of faith, by those who hold up a prophetic vision of a healed world.

So what are you going to do when you leave this place? How has this experience transformed you for action? Transformation can come in multiple forms—in prayer, in advocacy, in sharing resources and developing partnerships. Holding out the vision that God has planted within us, having the mind of God, is simply a form of prayer. We will want to add prayers for the courage and will to respond, the prayer of lament for the suffering that exists, and prayers of confession for our own complicity in that suffering, either by omission or commission.

A part of our response must be ongoing formation and education in our faith communities—about the prophetic tradition that motivates our action, about the reality of suffering around the globe, and about ways we can effectively respond as Christians. The gospels demonstrate the politically astute actions and tools Jesus uses—from his prophetic action in turning the tables in the Temple, to his calling of marginal and outcast people as his disciples, to his engagement with the powers at his own trial. Jesus the prophet was also a pretty effective community organizer, and he would encourage us to use the systems that oppress to better and creative ends, and when necessary to turn those systems on themselves. That is the deeply prophetic critique that underlies our scriptural tradition.

The immediate response of many when confronted by suffering in distant parts of the world is to send money. That is important, but it is not enough. Money without relationship can quickly become manipulation—either an attempted manipulation of our relationship with God, or a dismissal of the need to be involved. The great gift of a gathering like this is the opportunity to build relationships and partnerships with others—to see and know the gifts of each, and to understand that together we can accomplish far more than any of us alone. When God created humankind, God said, "It is not good for *Adham* to be alone." Unexpected things happen when we connect, when we begin to recognize and claim the body of God to which we belong. We are all changed in the process, and that very change begins to transform the world. The young people who gathered in and around this meeting have discovered that in concrete ways—they've seen the need of other young people in this place, have made some connections to the commonalities and differences in their own contexts, and all have been enriched and transformed. No one goes home unchanged.

We understand that all human beings are made in the image of God, and in our better moments, we also understand that loving God means doing justice for all who are made in God's image. Encouraging more of those "better moments" is one of the marks of mission we claim—forming Christians who are able and willing to set aside unholy self-interest for the sake of others. How do we begin to recognize that image of God in our neighbors, both near and far away? This meeting has been addressing two aspects of recognizing the image of God in our neighbor—both cultivating a compassionate response to suffering, and beginning to know the stranger seated next to us. Knowing the stranger—that Hebrew word "to know" (*yada*) is one of the most powerful in scripture—means entering into the stranger's life and learning its joys and sufferings, and, in the process, beginning to see the image of God. The bonds of affection born and nurtured here in Boksburg will continue to transform the larger world for a very long time to come. Because we have heard the cries of our brothers and sisters in Burundi or Sudan or South Africa or Nigeria, we can take that story home and share it with others, and help those cries in the wilderness be heard in our own communities. Each one of us will leave this place with new friends, new awareness of joy and suffering, and a larger image of the reality of God. This body of God, made of many and varied parts, can increasingly be understood as one. When we begin to see and experience that fundamental unity, we once again recognize the oneness of God. That is a great and abundant blessing, meant for larger life for the whole world.

Mahatma Gandhi put it this way: "May we become the change we hope for in the world." In Christian terms, that means becoming instruments of transformation, messengers and builders of new and abundant life.

Make us instruments of your peace and shalom in this world, O Lord. Where there is division, let us heal. Where there is hunger, let us be fed from the same table of your abundance. Where there is illness, motivate us to make well. Where there is ignorance, may we share your mind. Where there is oppression, let us liberate. And in all we do, may we build your community of shalom on this earth, to the glory of your name and your son, who came among us to heal the world.

Indeed, let us pray for the peace of Jerusalem, of every city that has no peace. Let us pray for a world where no one lives in fear, where enemies become friends, where the sun rises and the rain falls on all alike, who dwell in peace.

Chaos and Shalom—How to Change the World

Virginia Beach, Virginia, USA
Episcopal Communicators

25 April 2007

This group gathers annually to reflect on their common ministry, to learn, and to support each other. Earlier in the day we had joined a re-enactment of the first landing of European colonists, four hundred years earlier, on a beach nearby.

The job of communicators is to help to change the world through speech and images. Communication is a purposeful act—not just a reporting of what is, but the telling of a particular story for a particular purpose. Christians, at least in this corner of the church, claim that our purpose is reconciling the world, building the reign of God, restoring creation. The last time I checked, we were a long way from that grand dream. And that makes communication a prophetic task, which you and I share with many others, within this church as well as beyond it. The work of communicators has a parallel with the creative work of God, both at the beginning of creation and as God continues to call and urge and lure us into something that looks more like the divine goal of creation. We might understand that work as moving from chaos to shalom.

In the beginning when God created the heavens and the earth, the earth was a formless void and darkness covered the face of the deep, while a wind from God swept over the face of the waters.

That formless void is usually equated with chaos or nothingness, before God begins to breathe spirit over the waters or to speak the various parts of the cosmos into existence.

Then God said, "let there be light" and there was light. (Gen 1:1–3)

Divine speech begins to bring order out of chaos.

The great saga of origins continues after the beginnings of creation, through many generations of human beings. Knit throughout this story is the parallel re-entry of chaos—a retreat or departure from godly ways. Free will emerges very early, and comes to be an intrinsic part of the relationship between creator and created. The freedom to choose—that fruit of the tree of the knowledge of good and evil—comes to characterize all of creation. It is a necessary part of the story of salvation, from the choices of Eve and Adam, to the life and death of the utterly free human being Jesus, to the continuing existence of people and the rest of creation today. We cannot be either fully human or on the road to divinization without the ability to freely choose the good. Scientists would speak about the same sort of freedom in the rest of creation as the contingent nature of reality—without some indeterminacy, or unpredictability, life cannot evolve, nor can human beings develop consciousness.

Chaos has to do with the pre-creation lack of any recognizable or nameable structures, beings, or order. It also has to do with the creation's contingent and non-deterministic nature. But there is a third aspect to chaos that is an element of that contingency. Theologically, chaos can be understood as the potential for sin and the ability to choose evil, but it is also a necessary ingredient in the beauty and possibility of creation. Chaos in and of itself is a morally neutral realm of possibility. It's often understood in a popular sense to mean lack of order, or a declining degree of order, but all chaos has within it the possibility for a kind of evolving—or devolving—order whose results are unpredictable. Chaos can go either way—in a morally positive or a morally negative direction. In other words, with the chaos involved in creation you never know exactly what's going to happen until it happens. There is, however, a real tension with the understanding that repeated wrong or evil choices do lead to a world of greater entropy, and in the views of some, greater chaos. Yet, creation by itself cannot become either heaven or hell. It is only as human beings make creative or destructive choices that creation moves in one direction or the other.

Chaos is the *raison d'être* for religion. It is the motivation behind the human search for meaning, for relationship with something beyond ourselves. Chaos is what prompts the human desire to understand the nature of good and evil, and to predict or control the unpredictable. The underlying biblical assumption is the desire of God for a restored creation—human beings living at peace, in right relationship with one another, with God, and with the rest of God's creatures. All of salvation history is a quest for that ideal, that dream of God, which is only achieved through human interaction with the contingency of chaos. Human beings choosing the good become God's partners in building that vision of restored creation.

Chaos is also the basic driver behind the tradition of prophetic speech—language, story, and challenge that attempt to speak a new creation into existence. The prophetic tradition arises at a particular moment in history to confront social structures of injustice and oppression that subvert that dream of God. The Hebrew prophets speak both about what is wrong in society, and about what *right* would look like. Their speech, on behalf of God, is about a dream called *shalom*—more than mere peace, it is the kind of peace that is obtained when every person can enjoy the fruits of vineyard and orchard in abundance, when all have a blessed plenty, when no one suffers from disease or dies before the full and expected span of years, when no one cries aloud in grief or distress because all are healed and comforted. Isaiah's words speak of his prophetic vision:

> On this mountain the LORD of hosts will make for all peoples a feast of rich food, a feast of well-matured wines, of rich food filled with marrow, of well-matured wines strained clear. And he will destroy on this mountain the shroud that is cast over all peoples, the sheet that is spread over all nations; he will swallow up death forever. Then the Lord GOD will wipe away the tears from all faces . . . (25:6–8b)

That vision of all creation restored is taken up in later prophetic tradition as the kingdom of God, the reign of God, and it is the language of Jesus that is so profoundly challenging to the powers of his day. Even the language about the lion lying down with a lamb can easily be seen as an image of what human relationships would look like were they grounded in justice and mercy.

The prophets routinely speak against the kind of sinful and evil human behavior that deprives others of justice. Listen to Amos:

> Hear this, you that trample on the needy, and bring to ruin the poor of the land, saying, "When will the new moon be over so that we may sell grain; and the sabbath, so that we may offer wheat for sale? We will make the ephah small and the shekel great, and practice deceit with false balances, buying the poor for silver and the needy for a pair of sandals, and selling the sweepings of the wheat." (Amos 8:4–6)

The kind of willful destruction of human community and dignity that exploits the poor and defenseless is the most common subject of prophetic speech. The prophets routinely offer a different perspective of what Israel and her governors should be paying attention to, especially feeding the poor and caring for orphans, widows, and aliens. The needs of the least and last in the community, they insist, should be attended to first. The reason for doing so, repeated over and over again, is "because you were slaves in Egypt." God hears the cries of those who wander in the wilderness, seeking a new home, and God responds. Out of that horribly dehumanizing experience in Egypt comes a particular vocation to remember and care for others in like circumstances. The prophets remind Israel that all humanity is related. Israel may be a chosen people, but they have been chosen for the greater life of others. At a very important level, it is only the small details of history that have led some to the Promised Land and others into radical poverty. The great prophetic vision of universality that emerges in Isaiah proclaims that Israel exists for the world, and has a role in achieving that greater vision of possibility for all:

> "It is too light a thing that you should be my servant to raise up the tribes of Jacob and to restore the survivors of Israel; I will give you as a light to the nations, that my salvation may reach to the end of the earth." (Isa 49:6)

Jesus is equated with Wisdom's prophet in the gospels, and his deeds and words can be creatively understood in a prophetic framework:

> "For John the Baptist has come eating no bread and drinking no wine, and you say, 'He has a demon'; the Son of Man has come eating and drinking, and you say, 'Look, a glutton and a drunkard, a friend of tax collectors and sinners!' Nevertheless, wisdom is vindicated by all her children." (Luke 7:33–35)

> On the sabbath he began to teach in the synagogue, and many who heard him were astounded. They said, "Where did this man get all this? What is this wisdom that has been given to him? . . . And they took offense at him. Then Jesus said to them, "Prophets are not without honor, except in their hometown, and among their own kin, and in their own house." (Mark 6:2–4)

Throughout his ministry, Jesus finds ways of speaking for God about the dismal state of the world and the yet unmet possibilities of God's dream for creation—from the companions he chooses, to the parables he tells about the kingdom of God, to his cursing of fig trees and turning of tables. Even the scandals we call the incarnation and the resurrection make abundant sense in a prophetic framework, as God's response to those who cry in the wilderness. That pattern of divine attention to cries for help in the wilderness underlies all of what we call salvation history—and it's important to recognize that it's not over and done with at the last page of Revelation. God hears those cries of pain, and responds by continuing to lure us into a world that looks more like eternity, more like a heavenly banquet, more like God is Lord and not we ourselves. Chaos can be met, and transformed. Shalom can be the result.

The prophets God has continually given and sent us have an ability to speak clearly about the chaos that is and the shalom that could be. They include the great

Hebrew saints who cry out for justice in the gate, and offer a vision of what right relationship really looks like. Here is the way the prophet Micah puts it:

He has told you, O mortal, what is good; and what does the LORD require of you but to do justice, and to love kindness, and to walk humbly with your God? (6:8)

The great prophets of our tradition have usually been involved in major critique and change of socially accepted norms. William Wilberforce campaigned tirelessly for an end to the slave trade, as did others across the globe. That prophetic movement challenged the spiritual wisdom of its day that insisted that tradition upheld the continuation of slavery, and that slaves should obey their masters. The prophetic response offered a larger and more abundant vision of possibility that said all human beings are made in the image of God and deserving of full and equal dignity.

That tradition continues, for example with Paul Farmer, who insists that the rural poor in Haiti deserve the full blessings of medical attention, and with Greg Mortenson, who insists that equal access to education, for both girls and boys, will do more to make peace in Afghanistan than any weapon we can imagine. The prophetic tradition is not dead, indeed it rings through work that challenges the status quo around the world.

That prophetic tradition insists that full and abundant life is meant for all God's creatures, not just those who happen to live in prosperous communities or countries. Indeed, prosperity is not a blessing born out of holy living—the prophetic tradition always speaks against that kind of idolatrous self-focus. The prophetic tradition insists that each one of us is responsible for the flourishing of our brothers and sisters, wherever and however they now struggle to live. This tradition challenges all of us to speak truth to power, to say to our governments and to the world that there is something gravely and sinfully wrong with a world where the division between rich and poor continues to expand, where some live in palaces and recline on ivory couches while others starve outside the gates. Another prophet in our midst is Njongonkulu Ndungane, founder of Africa Monitor, a pan-African organization that tracks how the Western world meets its commitments to the MDGs and how recipient countries fulfil their part of the agreement. He expressed this prophetic vision most clearly when he said recently that while some starve, others are getting "stinking rich."

In our day, the prophets still speak for a world where the hungry are fed, the ill healed, all children educated, women and men treated equally, and no one is denied the basic necessities and dignities of life. The UN Millennium Development Goals are an important framework for what shalom might look like in our own day, and the Episcopal Church is increasingly focused on them as a basis for our work of building shalom and the reign of God.

We've looked at chaos as the initial stuff for creation, as the possibility to choose good or ill, as the injustice of the world that results when sinful, evil, or inadequate choices are made. We've looked at shalom as God's intent for a restored creation, as the possible dream for the world when compassion and justice have been put to work, when human beings make choices that consider the vast and interconnected web of reality that is creation, partnering with God on the route toward shalom. And we've considered the work of prophets as those who speak for the creative conversion of chaos into shalom.

But where are the prophets today? Who will speak those words? Who will do the work? Who will change the world from chaos to shalom?

I believe that each and every person sitting here—and every person who communicates faith—is capable of changing the world. Somewhere, somehow, each one of us has the capacity to tame the chaos around us and turn it toward the peace of shalom. Change agents come in many shapes and sizes, ages and abilities. Each one of us, inspired, can put some of the entropy back in the box. One of the principles of chaos theory is that very small changes in initial conditions can lead to radically different outcomes—consider, for example, the butterfly flapping its wings in China. What you or I do in this moment can bring hope and wholeness somewhere. The language and images we use can inspire and move others to be change agents themselves, and I firmly believe that is the charism of communicators. Proclamation, witness, storytelling, movie-making—all forms of communication are meant to move people.

Let me tell you about a change-agent named AJ. I knew AJ for five years or so. When I first met her, she was in her mid-forties, and she lived in a nursing home. I saw her every time I shared communion with the residents there. She had been paralyzed in an auto accident when she was in her early twenties, and she was the mother of a son who had grown up while she'd been living there. His picture graced the hallway where she spent much of her day in a kind of gurney-chair. She couldn't speak clearly, or move any part of her body coherently. But she had the world's most radiant smile. Her favorite hymn was "Amazing Grace" and she was a living example of that grace. She lived to bring joy to the people around her, and when she died after twenty-five years in that nursing home there were hundreds of people at her funeral—people whose lives had been richly blessed by her transforming presence.

Last week somebody pointed me to a poignant article in the most recent issue of *Glamour* magazine, about a young woman who has struggled for years with her identity as both a Christian and someone who has come to understand and accept herself as lesbian. She worked for years to redefine herself as ex-gay, without finding peace or success. Finally she joined the ranks of others who call themselves ex-ex-gay. She now seeks to support others who struggle to be both Christian and gay.

The route from chaos to shalom takes many forms. It can be about the condition of the heart and soul, about the body, or about the community. But most people only take that journey when they have others to lead them, offering vision, strength, and assurance that transformation is possible.

Linda Grenz, an educator and priest, tells a story of transformation that occurred in her congregation some twenty years ago. She has always insisted that you can't just tell people about Christianity or transformation—you have to help them experience it. Her congregation was interested in offering healing prayer with laying on of hands on Sunday morning, but rather than just starting to do it, they learned about prayer, listened to sermons about it, discussed it in Sunday school, and trained parents to pray with their children when they were ill. In the process, the congregation discerned who in their midst had gifts for healing and pastoral care, and a year later, when they had become a more intentionally praying community, they finally began to include laying on of hands in their Sunday morning worship.

One day Linda got a call from the parents of an eight-year-old boy who had just been diagnosed, at two different medical centers, with bone cancer. The physicians wanted to start aggressive treatment the next day, but the boy refused. "I want to go home," he insisted, "so Pastor Linda can pray for me first." The following Sunday morning, the boy and his parents presented themselves for prayer during the service. The story could end right there, and be a gracious example of how a congregation had learned to be and do hope for one of their members, how they had helped to bring peace in a small way to a young boy and his family. But the story goes on. The family went back to the hospital the following day, and another x-ray showed no trace of cancer. The doctors insisted somebody must have mixed up the other test results. Pastor Grenz says a young man came up to her years later, with his wife and child, and said, "This is the priest who taught us how to pray and believe in God."

Who changes the world? Those who equip and encourage others to make different choices. Claire Berry is a deacon in North Carolina whose focus is on helping others learn and do something about the MDGs in her diocese. She is persistence personified, nudging and needling folks to pay attention to suffering across the world—suffering they can do something about.

The children's ministry officer in the Episcopal Diocese of Oregon worked with the Lutheran Church to sponsor a children's advocacy day last Sunday. Their work is focused on domestic issues and the MDGs. They rented a big public square in downtown Portland, and advertised the event as *For Every Child, A Better World*, offering concrete examples of how individuals can move the world toward shalom for all children. This world would be a vastly different and more peaceful place if each child who is born had the basics of life—adequate food, shelter, medical care, education, and the care and nurture of a community.

Bowie Snodgrass is a twenty-something communicator in this Church. She is part of Transmission, which defines itself as "an underground Manhattan church founded in summer 2006 for ostracized Christians, agnostics, and bored churchgoers." Two weeks ago they sponsored Easter at Avalon. Avalon is a night-club in NYC that was originally built as Holy Communion Episcopal Church, by William Augustus Muhlenberg, in 1845. He is better known for beginning ministries that included employment agencies, English classes, schools, and medical services, and agencies to help brothel workers and abandoned mis-tresses start new lives. Transmission, which has also reached out to people of all kinds in today's New York, including sex workers, advertised their service with these words: "All are welcome, regardless of age, gender, profession, or how many times you've been born."

These change agents are all local communicators. They have all responded to particular circumstances in their own lives and neighborhoods. Like Jesus, they choose to walk around with the forgotten and ignored of this world. They are changing the world through the actions of individuals, through witness by word and example. If there is one thing that chaos theory teaches us, it is that small changes in initial conditions can result in massive differences in outcomes. Your ability to tell stories like these can inspire others to change the world.

There are a variety of ways in which individuals can effectively mobilize larger forces. Advocacy is one such essential choice for transformation. The MDGs will be accomplished by governmental giving for international development. And in this country, a rise to 1 percent of the federal budget is what's needed, which is several times current giving levels. As a nation, we have made significant com-mitments to AIDS work in Africa, and the advocacy of individuals has made our government a bit more generous than they might have been otherwise. But we have a long way to go. The draft of the 2008 budget is currently before Congress, and one version at least includes the promise of increased funding for that very kind of work. Advocacy is a reminder that our legislators work for us, and they pay atten-tion when constituents call, e-mail, or visit to remind them that we care about how our neighbors are faring in Zimbabwe, Sudan, or the Solomon Islands. As long as some live in abject poverty, we are all diminished. As long as so many have no food security, none of us will have physical security, whatever the Homeland Security folks try next at the airport. As long as young men and women here and across the world have no real possibility for education or meaningful employment, we will live under the looming shadow of war. None of us can say to another, we have no need of you. As John Donne said:

> *No man is an island, entire of itself . . .*
> *any man's death diminishes me . . .*
> *never send to know for whom the bell tolls, it tolls for thee.*

What can inspire us to hear that bell, to not only understand our interconnectedness, but to live differently as a result? And once comprehending and willing, how do we put that spirit into action? How do we urge chaos to become shalom?

In old-fashioned terms, I'm going to talk about virtue and character. In more contemporary language, we might call it a spirituality for transformation—or holy living as a leader. The task of transformation requires courage, creativity, and connection.

We have to begin with courage, the willingness to speak truth and take challenging stands. That is an essential part of the prophetic charism. It is related to the virtue of humility, for we must be willing to get out of our own way so that the word we proclaim may be a godly one and not ours alone. It would seem to be the native province of the kind of communicators you are. Courage comes with practice, and the sort of athletic training that Paul talks about. It cannot be an arrogant sort of attitude, but comes from the authority of knowing who one is—and to whom one belongs. Christians would say that it is the result of knowing oneself beloved of God.

The willingness to risk confronting structures of power and oppression may be the most daunting part of leadership, but it's the most essential. We know the story of what challenging those powers can produce, and we've just lived through it again. Yes, it can bring trial, torture, and death, but that is never the final word. Even—especially—the chaos of Holy Week contains the possibility and promise of transformation.

Courage comes in a myriad of forms, beginning with the mundane: the willingness to gently challenge a litterbug or a parent applying undue force to a misbehaving child. The ability to challenge a self-serving legislator or other public official. The willingness to admit one's own error. Courage also means looking within, and challenging the parts of ourselves that we might rather just leave alone. It means hearing the angel say to us, "Fear not, for I am always with you."

Have courage. Think outside the box—even if we haven't done it that way before! Honor the gifts and dignity of those whom polite society would rather ignore.

Nellie Greene is a deacon at Chestnut Hill United Methodist Church. Her story was in the *Philadelphia Inquirer* just before Easter.[4] This is what she says about herself, after describing her education and degrees:

Due to severe brain damage from a car accident on my way to college in 1970, I am legally blind and a wheelchair user, and I use a spelling board for communication. My mission is to encourage, enlighten, and inspire all whom I meet, especially the elderly and people with disabilities, to be responsible to each other, the earth, and all sentient beings with compassion and humor, so they will know in their heart they matter and are deeply cherished by their God.[5]

Along with the newspaper article, there was a video of a powerful dance and poem presentation by an actor speaking for Nellie and dancing with her in her wheelchair. It demonstrates the courage of both Nellie and the dancer who uses her art to speak for her.

A change agent has to value creativity, even to the point of playfulness. If we understand ourselves as made in the image of God, then that image must certainly include the ability to speak things into existence—or at least to take mud and spit and begin to make something out of it. The solution to today's challenge is probably not identical to yesterday's challenge, even though there may be some continuity. If we already knew how to solve it, it wouldn't be a challenge, after all. This kind of creativity also has its roots in courage—the willingness to try something new and untried, to think outside that old box, or even to hold an established position lightly—which is also related to humility. The creative spirit can see connections, find common ground, and build a greater unity among people or positions that at first glance seem remarkably disparate.

That sense of interconnectedness, or fundamental unity, is an underlying or guiding principle in a spirituality of leadership. It grows out of compassion, or perhaps gives rise to it, knowing that each part of this cosmos is dependent in deep and mysterious ways on every other part. There is a wonderful image in Hinduism called Indra's net. It is something like a vast fishnet, with a jewel at each intersection of the web. Each of those jewels reflects every other, forming something like a hologram. When we begin to see ourselves as one such jewel, reflecting, and therefore involved in, every other, we begin to respond differently. You do that kind of reflecting work each time you offer a vision of hope, a story about where God is at work, an invitation to enter the suffering of others.

We know that we are part of a larger whole, and if we live as though that were of central truth and importance, we just might reduce the urge to see our own desires as all-important. The great tragedy of sociopaths is their inability to empathize with the suffering of another. The actions of the disturbed young man at Virginia Tech tell that story in abundance—rejected and spat upon, he responded with violence. At least some of the people around him recognized that wound in him, and reached out. We will never know what might have shifted his experience toward healing. For it is when we know ourselves beloved—in the deep, visceral, biblical sense of the word—and know that others are equally beloved, that we can experience the hunger of a child in India as our own, and become far more willing to reach out and feed that child, and change a world that keeps so many hungry.

That compassionate sense of connection can lead us to value the gifts of all parts of the community, to connect in ways that do no violence to another's identity or dignity. The New Testament imagery of the Body of Christ is about connectedness, and the need for all the parts of the Body to be valued and esteemed in order for the whole to be healthy and effective. That sense of connection is what is beginning to awaken the peoples of this world to the enormous tragedy of climate change. When we begin to understand that our carbon use here will likely drown the habitations of people in the South Pacific before much longer, when we begin to recognize the pain of people whose homes and livelihoods are fast disappearing, we just might find the courage to act.

Our actions will require both courage and creativity, for we are long established in patterns that have led us to this point. We will have to learn and re-learn how to choose wisely and well, to choose in ways that consider the suffering of our sisters and brothers as well as our own. It will take the best and most creative kinds of communication to urge us all in more constructive and life-giving directions. We'll need the prophetic ability to speak about dissatisfaction with received wisdom and the current state of the world, as well as the prophetic word of hope, and the possibility of life abundant meant for each.

The good news is that this prophetic work is going on all around us, as seeds growing secretly—and not so secretly. You and I have the ability to change this world into something that looks more like that great dream of God, that great and glorious vision of shalom. The task of communicators is to challenge the injustice and death-dealing realities around us, and to inspire and encourage others to build toward God's dream of shalom, of life more abundant, not only for ourselves but for each and every human being and creature in the cosmos. I give thanks for your passion and persistence in speaking as God's prophets.

Religion and Violence: Untangling the Roots of Conflict

New York, New York, USA
Trinity Institute

21 January 2008

This conference focused on religion and violence; the texts for this sermon were drawn from the scripture of the three Abrahamic faiths.

Scripture from each tradition was read:
Joshua 24:14–18; John 3:1–12; Surah al-Ma'ida (5):48

How do we hear these texts? As Jews, Christians, or Muslims, do we hear only our own tradition?

Do we hear with the ears of one who has been liberated from slavery? Then, choose this day to serve the God who has done that.

Do we hear what we have always heard, justification for where we are, what we believe, the community in which we live and move and have our comfortable being? Careful—nobody gets to see the kingdom of God without being born again.

Do we hear with the assumption that we have the full and final and only truth? Well, God is still at work—don't be too eternally certain.

At their best, religious traditions have always sought to lead human beings into greater understanding and knowledge of the divine. Each of the world's great religions was birthed in a unique context and time, yet each affirms a truth that reaches beyond that limited context. It is as though a community, living in its own valley, looks around for generations, mines the wisdom of its holy sages over the centuries, seeing and seeking truth in that place, and yet intuiting that there is a larger application for that truth. The great religions for long periods worked in their own valleys, and a few adventurers scaled the peaks and ridges between those valleys and confirmed that truth in a larger perspective. Most of humanity, however, continues to affirm that one valley's truth is the whole truth.

It is much like the differing scales and theoretical methods of physicists. Newtonian physics works well at the human scale. Quantum physics is far more appropriate at much smaller scales, and relativistic and other kinds of physics are needed at the cosmic scale. Does that make any of them untrue? Despite the quest of centuries, we don't yet have a Theory of Everything.

The frequent human assumption that one cultural and religious context is the whole, and the hubris or idolatry involved in that assumption, become the underpinning of religiously sanctioned violence. The self-justified claim of truth, whether religious or otherwise, is the source of all violence. If I am the most important reality in the universe, then my desires are certainly to be satisfied, whatever may stand in my way. The use of force to meet those desires is the definition of violence. Violence has its verbal origins in the same root as vital, "having to do with life." But violence is the use of one's own life force to subvert or traduce the life of another.

The nature of religion, hinted at in the roots of the word—"to tie together" or "to link to something larger"—is to provide a worldview that is effective in leading us beyond ourselves, enabling us to give our hearts to something larger than our own narrow self-interest. The great religious traditions insist that our relationship with that larger something or someone is reflected in our relationship with our fellow human beings. Religion can stop, however, at the binding of a like-minded community that is unable to see beyond its own group. That is the religion of the valley-bound, who see all outsiders as at least somewhat demonic. It is the religion of the enslaved, and it is the religion of those who will not engage another who also claims eternal truth.

Each of the sacred texts we have heard this night has hints of getting us out of our riverine declivity. Torah tells us the God to be worshiped is the one who delivers us from the slavery of domination, whether by Pharaoh or multinational corporation or mindless obedience. Jesus reminds us we must be born from above, into some larger divine reflection, in order to see what God's world really looks like and is truly meant to be. The Koran hints that while we are not only or yet one people, in that very diversity God is at work, and bids us strive to outdo one another in righteousness.

These three great faith traditions are far from harmonious, at least on the valley floor. Yet they share a foundational assumption that the end of things is about peace—that great peace that reaches through or beyond human suffering to shalom, salaam, Islam. Each of these faith traditions speaks of that dream or end of God in different images, yet there is a transcendent urge toward human community where all are fed in abundance, where no one studies war any more, where swords are reforged into tools to feed the hungry. Each faith urges on us the awareness that our relationship with those around us is, in vastly important ways, the relationship we have with the source of all: *baruch atah Adonai eloheinu, melech ha'olam.*[6]

At our best, we might even manage to affirm that the water flowing through these three Abrahamic valleys has a common origin and source, and returns to the same oceanic reality.

Violence results when we lose sight of that larger reality, whether in the person next to us or the folk in the next valley.

The reminders about that larger reality come from the prophets and mystics in all our traditions. The sad truth is that most adherents know little of either prophetic or mystical tradition. Too often we are caught up either in scrupulous but dry adherence to rules or in impassioned but mindless ecstasy. But to embrace the fullness of life for which we were created, we must learn to love God and neighbor with our whole being, with mind, heart, soul, and means.

The Hasidic tradition speaks of that need for loving with both mind and heart; Rabbi Nachman of Breslau said: "Do not think that the words of prayer as you say them go up to God. It is not the words themselves that ascend; rather it is the burning desire of your heart that rises like smoke to heaven. If your prayer consists only of words and letters, but does not contain your heart's desire, how can it rise up to God?"

We remember today the birthday of a prophet who was also something of a mystic, a man who sought to deliver his people from Pharaoh, who knew himself born from above even though he had feet of clay, who, at least toward the end, was not loath to make common cause with his brothers and sisters in other faith traditions. Martin Luther King, Jr. went to the mountain top, looked out over those other valleys, and did not come down again before he went home, dead by violence. Yet the antidote to violence is always more life.

As the Sufi mystical poet Hafez said in the fourteenth century, "What is the sign of those who know God? 'Dear, they have dropped the knife. They have dropped the cruel knife most so often use upon their tender selves and others.'"

Those who drop the knife have done as the writer of 1 John suggests—they have given up fear: "Perfect love casts out fear, for fear has to do with punishment, and whoever fears has not reached perfection in love" (1 John 4:18). The end of violence is discovering the wild embrace of the one who has created us.

Rabi'a of Basra, an eighth-century Sufi saint, speaks of fear and love:

Ironic, but one of the most intimate acts of our body is death. So beautiful appeared my death—knowing who then I would kiss, I died a thousand times before I died. "Die before you die," said the Prophet Muhammad. Have wings that feared ever touched the Sun? I was born when all I once feared—I could love.[7]

The Christian mystic Meister Eckhardt put it like this in the fourteenth century: "They are always kissing, they can't control themselves. It is not possible that any creature can have greater instincts and perceptions than the mature human mind. God ripened me. So I see it is true: all objects in existence are wildly in love."[8]

And Rumi, the Sufi mystic: "With passion pray. With passion work. With passion make love. With passion eat and drink and dance and play. Why look like a dead fish in the ocean of God?"[9]

Dead fish have been hooked—by violence. The response to the violence of our faith communities is either to tap the knowledge that comes from scaling the heights, those ridges between our river valleys, or to jump in the river and swim down to the sea. But not as a dead fish.

Encountering Peace

Brasilia, Brazil
7 July 2007

This visit to the Igreja Episcopal-Anglicana do Brasil took us to three of the largest population centers—Brasilia, Rio de Janeiro, and Sao Paolo. We found a church energetically engaged in mission with the "least of these." This sermon was preached twice, once in Spanish and once in English.

Isaiah 6:1–8; Ps 126; John 20:19–23

Why were the doors locked that lonely evening? What were the disciples afraid of? At some level they must have been worried that the authorities would come for them and do to them what they had just done to Jesus. It is not unlike what happens even today to revolutionaries or those who work on behalf of the poor. Were the disciples afraid they would be "disappeared" in the middle of the night, or go onto someone's death list, or become public examples of what happens when you confront an occupying government or a structure of injustice?

Or were those disciples still stunned at what had happened, unable to make any decision about what to do next?

In either case, there they sat, paralyzed with fear or indecision, until Jesus appeared in their midst. He confronted their fear by showing them his wounds, and reminding them that even death cannot prevail. Then he told them to be at peace, and sent them out.

Something similar happened to Isaiah. He had a remarkable and awesome experience of the reality of God that produced in him a sense of utter unworthiness. He began to respond by saying that he couldn't possibly live with that awareness. But he, too, was given peace, and then sent out to do God's work.

Have you ever been in a situation like that? Terrorized or paralyzed either by fear or your own incapacity?

In early 2000 I was on sabbatical, and I spent part of it driving around the western United States, visiting a number of congregations and dioceses that were engaged in developing total baptismal ministry. I visited a congregation in Nevada and had several conversations, and as I was leaving, the priest said to me, "What you have done here is very much like what a bishop does during a visit. Can I offer your name in the election process for bishop here?" I laughed and said to her, "That makes no sense at all. I'm too young, I'm a woman, and besides, I haven't been the rector of a big fancy congregation. That's ridiculous." And I left and drove across Nevada in a snow storm.

But God did not let go of me. As I continued that trip, the idea that priest had planted would not go away. It began to truly terrify me. I was reminded of what it says in Hebrews (10:31): "It is a fearful thing to fall into the hands of the living God." But by the time I got home I had found a measure of peace. Even though the idea made no sense to me, I understood that I was being asked to put my fears and incapacity away and say yes to the process. That one part of the decision was all I had to tackle. Truly the rest was up to God.

How do we move from paralysis or fear to action? How do we respond to that call to go out into the unknown? Those who first brought the gospel to this part of the world undoubtedly came in great fear and trepidation. Yet they had heard a voice sending them out into new worlds, and they had found enough peace to venture forth. All they had to do was to say yes to the invitation to go.

The work that is asked of each one of us—to participate in God's mission of healing the world—puts fear into most of us, if we're honest. It is an enormous and awesome and impossible job. If we were entirely conscious of the evil and injustice that we will encounter, we would be even more afraid. Yet we continue to go, most of us, every day, to build the reign of God—one encounter and one person at a time.

Several of us had the remarkable opportunity in Brasilia to meet the government's Minister of the Environment. She has passion and certainty about her work, and she is clear that it has to do with bringing peace—the kind of peace that is only born of justice. A peace that will offer more abundant life to those who struggle without, and a peace that will consider the rest of creation and our responsibility to be stewards of this garden.

Our ability to go out and do this work of God is rooted in that same sense of peace and relationship that the disciples received from Jesus, and that Isaiah received from his heavenly vision: "Peace be with you. As God has sent me, so I send you." "Receive Holy Spirit and go out there and build a world of peace."

Where do we encounter that peace? Certainly the community that gathers week by week is part of it, the incarnate reminder of God's love for each one of us. The utter graciousness of reality is part of it as well, the endless reminders of God's presence in the wonderful and challenging people all around us. And the promise of new life born even in the face of death—a promise we see enfleshed all around us. There is abundant reason for peace, if we have eyes to see it and hearts to recognize it.

Our ability to be peace in the world grows out of our own experience of knowing peace, even and especially in the face of fear.

What are we afraid of? What hinders us from saying yes to God's dream of a healed world? Is it believing that we have to have all the answers or that we have to tackle the whole world? It is primarily a matter of saying yes to the invitation to get up and go.

Whom can God send, and who will go for us?

The prayer of our hearts, the yearning we share, is that we be able to say, "Here am I, send me." May we be able to say, "Give me your peace, and send me."

May God's peace be in our hearts, and God's peace be the product of our hands, and hearts, and minds.

Remembrance, Recognition, and Reconciliation

Jamestown, Virginia, USA
Second Decade of Remembrance, Recognition, and Reconciliation
All Saints

1 November 2007

A gathering of Native Americans from across the continent, to reaffirm the Jamestown Covenant. We gathered in the open air, near the reconstructed first Anglican chapel on this continent, for Eucharist.

Ecclesiasticus 44:1–10, 13–14; Psalm 149;
Revelation 7:2–4 ,9–17; Matthew 5:1–12

We are here to remember, recognize, and reconcile the native peoples of this land and those who have come after. We begin here a second decade of this work, work that is centuries late, long overdue, and far from finished.

There is something wonderfully appropriate about recommitting to this work on the feast of All Saints, a time to remember all the faithful who have come before us, all of those who have loved God and lived in a way that shows that love to others. That passage from Ecclesiasticus was written for a context far away and many centuries before our own, but it is as pertinent today as it was twenty-two hundred years ago. About whom does this speak? The ancestors of its author, Jesus ben Sirach? Older Jewish worthies? The elders who lived on these shores? The ancestors of immigrants—who? Gather up your memories of those who have come before us.

Let us now praise famous men—and women:

- who ruled kingdoms, made a name by their valor, gave sound advice, spoke in oracles,

- who led people by their counsels and knowledge of the people's lore

- who were wise in words of instruction

- who composed musical tunes, or set down ballads

Some have left behind a name. Of others there is no memory
Can you identify your holy ancestors in those descriptions of saints?

I am aware of some who have left behind a name—or sometimes several names, depending on who is doing the calling. Many of those whose names we know today were bridge people, who labored in some way to reconcile divisions between their people and the immigrants who brought so many challenges and changes.

- Wahunsunacock, or Chief Powhatan, who gathered and led the nations in Tenomakah, this part of what is now called Virginia. He was one of the first to interact with the settlers here in Jamestown.

- His daughter Matoaka, better known as Pocahontas, who made an alliance with John Rolfe, was baptized Rebecca Rolfe and bore a son who is still claimed as ancestor by many in these parts.

- Thocmentony, or Sarah Winnemucca, the first Native American woman to publish in English, who spoke tirelessly on behalf of her Paiute people, native to what is now northern Nevada and eastern Oregon.

- Black Elk, or Hehaka Sapa, Lakota teacher of wisdom, who taught many generations about Christianity and about his vision of native spirituality.

- Chief Sealth (Ts'ial-la-kum), whose words challenged our forebears to care for this earth, and continue to challenge us today.

- Sacagawea (or Sakakawea), Shoshone guide to the Lewis and Clark expedition, and father of Jean Baptiste Charbonneau, another bridge person. He studied in Europe, spoke half a dozen languages at least, and labored for a time as alcalde (mayor) of Misión San Luis Rey in San Diego. He lost his position because of the passion he brought to his work on behalf of the Native people there.

There are others whose names are known only to their most direct descendants, and there are many whose deeds we remember and recognize, even though their names have been lost:

- the politically wise, who built the Iroquois and Algonquin confederacies, and taught the English settlers something about governance

- the Apache, whose adaptability let them successfully resist Spanish incursion for more than two hundred years

- the Paiute, who are among the oldest Episcopal communities in Nevada. They received the gospel, and continue to work to indigenize it. The Navajo are doing the same kind of bridge-building work

Remembering and recognizing the saints among us is often a matter of telling the stories. Those saints are all around us if we can notice. In the last couple of days, I noticed these who seem to me to be saints:

- Sister Miriam, who provides the kind of strengthening that's meant in that old word "comfort," and who asks probing questions and gives sound counsel

- the court reporter who records a deposition cheerfully and with interest

- the Asian woman I sat behind on the train—deep in meditation, quiet and reverent

- the preacher I heard through an open door last weekend, proclaiming a wonderfully true insight: "Prayer and fasting go together like red beans and rice"

- the cheerful conductors on the train, who offered their greeting as they punched my ticket

- the sewer worker in his traffic-repelling orange jacket, joking with his buddy in the truck across the street: "You can't buy me a cup of coffee!"

What saints do you remember? Can you recognize others you haven't thought of as saints before? There are some whose names we learn, and others whose names we will never know.

Our ancestors who brought us to this day—both the ones whose names and stories we know, and the other, faithful ones who gave life to others, and are now forgotten.

The many unnamed, particularly women and others marginalized by dominant cultures, whose witness and weary labor made it possible for you and me to be called to work that would have been unthinkable a generation ago.

Remember the many searchers after justice who continue to challenge systems that keep some in thrall while others prosper—Martin Luther King, Desmond Tutu, Aung San Suu Kyi, Vine Deloria, Jr.

Saints are bridge builders, strengthening our awareness of the connections between the sacred and the everyday. Saints do that in reconciling relationships between peoples. When we tell their stories, and bring them to mind, we build a bridge that permits their gifts to be used once again, in this age.

Remember the saints who have come before us, recognize the gifts they have given so abundantly to those who follow, and join in reconciling both their stories and the need for saints in our day. Ten years from now, God willing, may we have a clearer sense of our common roots, and the bridge we can build to a common future.

Towards Peace in Korea

Paju/Seoul, South Korea
Opening Eucharist
16 November 2007

TOPIK is an ongoing effort toward peace-making on the Korean peninsula. The now-retired archbishop of Korea gathered Anglicans from several parts of the globe to talk about peace-making. He asked me, as representative of the American church, and the archbishop of Japan to accompany him on a pilgrimage to North Korea (Geumgansang) before this consultation began.

Micah 4:1–5; Psalm 85:7–13; Ephesians 2:13–18; Matthew 5:43–48

"Love your enemies and pray for those who persecute you" (Matt 5:44). We have gathered here to do just that, and to work at tearing down the barriers between us that make enemies. We are here to practice peace-making, to un-learn our ability to make war, to shape communities that seek peace and harmony rather than division.

We are here to affirm the peace that is ours in Christ. We are here to re-member, re-call, re-collect the pieces of broken human community, that they might be fully restored in Christ. The members of this body are one, even though we too easily forget and work against that reality. When you and I gather around this holy table of word and meal, when we gather beyond this room for conversation, for meals, and for fellowship, we begin to re-member the reality in which we already exist. May our prayer be that whatever clouds our memory be blown utterly away.

That great image of nations streaming to Zion to worship the one God in peace should challenge us. We cannot look around to find a full and perfect example anywhere in this world—there is too much corruption, too much selfishness, too much strife in every city and nation around us. Yet there is also hope, and glimpses of human community restored, if we are willing to look. However tentative and imperfect, peace has come in South Africa, peace has arrived in Ireland, peace is being built one school at a time in Afghanistan, and peace may yet emerge in the Middle East.

This gathering can be a witness to that possibility. Wherever people begin to look for the image of God in people they would rather see as enemy, Zion emerges from the mist, and the nations begin to stream toward that holy mountain. The Truth and Reconciliation Commission of South Africa is a mountain of peace toward which the nations are indeed streaming.

Wherever people gather in councils of peace, rather than war, God's instruction bears fruit. This gathering has the potential to be another such witness to God's holy mountain. May teaching go forth from here to bring peace in every corner of the world.

Whenever people ask how a nuclear reactor may be an instrument of peace, how it can produce energy and treat cancer, rather than fashion weapons of war, there the Spirit of God is at work. When food and medical care and education are shared with those who have none, instruction is going out from Zion.

Yet this is never a passive process. We can't just sit and wait for the Spirit to work alone. You and I, and everyone we meet in our daily rounds, can share in that work of the Spirit. Each one of us can engender change, can forge weapons into instruments of peace. And when we move together in the power of the spirit, the earth begins to move as well.

That work of shifting the ground begins with our own attitudes, responses, and actions. How do we perceive the stranger—as threat or as the image of God? There is a part of each one of us that awakens to full alert at the presence of a stranger, an unknown, one who is "other." That reaction is an instinctual survival skill, and in itself is neither good nor evil. But what we do with that heightened awareness is a moral decision. When we become profoundly aware of the presence of "the other" we are confronted with a series of choices. Is this other a threat or a potential blessing—or do we need to gather more information before we decide? We might do well to remember that the unknown stranger just might be a divine messenger—an angel. I am convinced that every such stranger may bear a divine message if we can discover and receive it. Certainly every encounter brings an image of God, an image we do not yet know, and that meeting must therefore be rich with creative possibility.

What divine messages have been received in our time in Geumgangsan? Where and in whom did we meet God anew? How will we discover an unknown image of God in this meeting? That divine image is most certainly here, all around us, and we can find it more readily when we receive the stranger with openness and even vulnerability.

The choice between vulnerability and fear underlies the human ability to make both peace and war. That choice is what most profoundly underlies Jesus' witness, and his life, death, and resurrection. Living in radical openness to the image of God in the other may lead to death, but it is also the only route to full and abundant life.

The human ability to make war has mostly to do with fear: People and their leaders live in fear of their neighbors or what they may do. Some use fear to control others and fill their own desires. Some live in fear of territorial expansion, or lack of access to resources and the basic stuff of life—like water, fuels, cropland, or fisheries. Neighbors may live in fear of reprisals for old injustices—like Jacob and Esau, or Israel and Palestine. If we do not settle or forgive those old disputes, we will continue to live with fear.

Living in fear only degrades life, for it leads inexorably to violence. Living in fear denies the fundamental hope we share, for it condemns us to remain in the grave of the past. Christians are not meant to live in fear. We are born anew in hope for a dream that we expect will become reality. That great dream of God is for a restored and reconciled creation. We make peace now so that God's cosmic dream may be made real. Jesus says, "Love your enemy" now, in the present, so that we might "be perfect as God is perfect." That perfection is a becoming, undergirded by reconciling work in this age, luring us on toward the vision of all creation existing in the full presence and perfection of God.

Peace-making requires confronting fear, both our own fear and the fear that keeps others in that grave. Loving our enemies means letting go of our fear of their perceived difference, letting go of our fear that they will take something precious from us, letting go of our fear that they intend only evil toward us. Loving our enemies means insisting that each is made in the image of God, that each of us can live in peace only when all live under their own fig trees, with vines bent low and heavy with fruit. Loving our enemies means insisting that there is abundance for all in God's great dream of a restored creation.

To make peace, we must feed all our neighbors, both stranger and friend, with the same gusto with which we feed our own children. We must seek the welfare of all with the same energy we spend to provide education and health care for our own families. Loving our enemies is only another version of loving our neighbors, for in truth all God's creatures are neighbors. We do not have the luxury of distinguishing stranger from neighbor or friend. Setting down our swords and spears, and remaking them into tools for farming or learning or healing means we must meet those neighbors in all their diversity and see only the beloved image of God.

May this gathering invite us to see the image of God we all share, even when that image is tainted with fear and enmity. May we be transformed in this meeting, so that we may go forth and transform the world. May God's peace be made real, may the shalom of God spread forth from Zion—no, may it speed forth from Zion. May God's peace spread over this earth like the blessing of rain cloud in the desert.

Leading the Flock

Cuddesdon, England
Transforming Episcope
Ripon College

10 July 2008

This address was to a conference dedicated to considering the ministry of bishops, particularly as women in England begin to see the process toward the episcopate opened to them. The conference began just a couple of days after England's synod voted to begin the process toward permitting women to serve as bishops.

Well, I'm glad I don't have to tend to a funeral tonight. It doesn't even look like hospice care is going to be required. But your process toward women bishops looks like a very long slog. It will take continued leadership in many arenas, and it will require your persistence, hope, and confidence.

I know you're going to hear what I say tonight through ears tuned to particular issues. I invite you beyond those particularities to think about Christian leadership in a broad and general sense. If you want to bring those two together strategically, the Spirit usually finds abundant room to work.

The word "leader" comes from roots that mean "to go or travel." That usage assumes we know where we're going; in order to lead, we have to have a goal in mind. That goal or vision is held up alongside what we know of present reality to produce tension. There's an eschatological piece, a prophetic piece, to leadership, because it says, "If we're not there yet, then something will have to change." In shorthand, leadership is about motivating change.

Pastoral leadership, in the biblical sense, is about leading the flock to food, water, healing, and peace. It begins with those great visions of a banquet on a hillside; a community of shalom where the hungry are fed, the blind see, and the prisoners set free. Jesus claims that great tradition as his own mission statement in the fourth chapter of Luke, when he goes into the synagogue and reads from Isaiah:

The Spirit of the Lord is upon me, because he has anointed me to bring good news to the poor. He has sent me to proclaim release to the captives and recovery of sight to the blind, to let the oppressed go free, to proclaim the year of the Lord's favor. (4:18–19)

And then he sits down and says, "Today this scripture has been fulfilled in your hearing." That is the great vision, and the part that proclaims that we're on the way—today!

When Jesus meets the disciples for breakfast after the resurrection, what does he tell these budding leaders? "Feed my lambs . . . tend my sheep . . . feed my sheep" (John 21:15–17). That's our job—to lead them to good pasture and clean water, to care for the weak and sick, to keep the flock safe from predators, or teach the wolves to eat lettuce. Without a shepherd, the flock is likely to scatter and die. And without leaders, nothing changes for the good, nothing moves toward that vision of a restored and healed world. So, in Christ's name, take up his vision, and help lead the world toward it.

A lot of pastoral work has to do with equipping the flock to be leaders themselves. After all, the baptized may all be sheep, but they also have a vocation to be shepherds—every single one of us. I'll call that "baptismal leadership" as a way of talking about our baptismal vocation to follow Jesus, working to heal the world. Every baptized person is called to leadership somewhere, particularly to that work of motivating change, in some part of his or her life.

We all have a part in the mission of God, whatever language you want to use for it—reconciling the world, *tikkun olam*, shalom, the heavenly banquet. We have been blessed with different gifts, none more important than another. As Paul is so fond of saying, the body has many parts, which when working together, can help build up the whole. The hard thing to remember in that image is that the body of Christ already has a head—and it's not any one of us.

This kind of leadership is servant leadership—being friends of Jesus serving others. It is needed in every facet of life: for our own internal work, in our intimate communities, at work, in the larger community, the civic square, in our leisure and sabbath time, in the world, and in the church. There is no part of our existence which has fully realized the reign of God. Nor is anything beyond the reach of God. And that leadership challenge is to hold up the disconnect, and begin to motivate ourselves and others toward the vision and dream of God.

The ordained model that kind of leadership, but they don't do all the work. There aren't enough deacons and priests and bishops, for one thing, and the reality is that the ordained spend far too much of their time within the institution to have deep and abiding impacts on most of the other spheres of daily existence.

Diaconal leadership is about motivating the baptized for service based on their gifts, and about speaking a prophetic word to the church about the poor and hungry, the sick and the prisoners. Presbyteral leadership has most to do with equipping and feeding the saints—feed my sheep, again—for their work in daily life. And episcopal leadership is about proclaiming that great vision of the reign of God —at its root, it is the apostolic task for which each baptized person is sent.

Episcopal leadership is about the big picture. That's why it's called oversight. I remember standing on a hill in Kenya with the bishop of Machakos, surveying the beauty of the green countryside, and joking about that: Were we going to oversee this work or overlook it? Indeed, there are times for overlooking some goings-on in a diocese, in the spirit of benign neglect, or ignoring little things that are distractions. But most of the ministry of oversight is about learning to think in terms of the body as a system of interconnected parts, who all need to function well. Good functioning has a great deal to do with truth-telling, for how can the body function if the parts are not honest and direct about their joys and anguish? And for the body to function well, the parts must be continually urged to build and maintain healthy connections and relationships.

The Latin word for bishop, *pontifex*, points to the essential nature of bridge-building in episcopal ministry. And that bridge-building work has increasing importance today—not just with disaffected parts of our own body, but with other bodies that share our vision and values. How can we collaborate with groups who share our concern that the hungry be fed? They don't have to be Christian, and they don't have to express any particular religious claim; they simply have to care about feeding the hungry. God can use those beyond our normal sphere of influence to do godly work. God always has—that's certainly what the long history of outsiders is about in salvation history. Remember the big battle over whether Gentiles could be part of this body? We can all give thanks that the early church was able to see a larger vision.

The task of leadership grows out of that ability to see a larger vision and hold it up in contrast to what is. It's essentially about change and transformation, not institutional preservation—that is the function of management. Yes, leaders in this institution usually need some capability as managers, but it is a sorry church that thinks there's no reason to change anything —pretty soon, that leads to a dead church.

The important thing is that all the baptized share in leadership. Diaconal ministry: what do you think of? Caring for sick, feeding the hungry, urging parishioners to become involved in those ministries? But that kind of ministry is the work of every baptized person, and when the baptized take up that ministry, transformation happens. When you work with the sick and the hungry and the marginalized, you start to ask questions. You may wonder why so many people who work at the local factory are getting sick, or why there are hungry and homeless people in a prosperous nation. When you start asking those questions, not only do you elicit resistance, but you begin to wake people up to the need for social change, which in this society happens most easily at the ballot box. The very resistance to status quo is a gospel moment. As Dom Helder Camara noted several decades ago, "When I feed people they call me a saint, when I ask why there are so many hungry people, they call me a communist." Why *did* the early church communities insist that goods should be held in common?

Consider priestly ministry. Whether ordained to the priesthood or not, every single baptized person is called to priestly leadership—the kind of leadership that's all about reconciliation. Like children who learn how to settle a quarrel on the playground, or like mediators who learn how to heal religious division, or people who work to motivate the public to work for peace, this is leadership work we all share, but it's supported, taught, encouraged, and even motivated by icons of that kind of leadership—as they gather the members of the body around the banquet table.

What about episcopal ministry? It is not about teaching everyone in church to wear an apron and gaiters—though that's an idea. Maybe bishops just have to convince one wing of the church that real bishops wear aprons and stockings, and did in this country for many years!

Episcopal ministry is about fostering a bigger-picture view, so that all the baptized begin to make decisions that consider the effects on people far away in time or space. Why is it important to steward the resources of the earth? Why should a retired person care about the educational system for children across the country or in Bangladesh? How do we form Christians who routinely think about planning for succession, not just in thinking of the church when they write their wills, but in how their ministry in the workplace is preparing for those who will follow? Those are all forms of episcopal ministry, and all those who are baptized are called to it.

Perhaps the current struggle over women bishops in this country has a lot to do with the understanding in many parts of the church that these kinds of ministry and leadership are reserved to the (male) ordained. If we had a more pervasive understanding of baptism as ministry and a calling to transformational leadership, I don't think we'd be having these arguments. We probably wouldn't be having them with certain wings in the church if we read our Bibles more carefully, particularly the parts about Mary of Magdala, the apostle to the apostles, and the Syrophoenician woman, and the Samaritan woman at the well, and Lydia and Prisca, and the other women who were clearly leaders in the early church. It's when we turn ministry and leadership into secret knowledge, and misread the words of Jesus to insist that he's only revealed these secrets to a few, that we struggle.

The church is just a laboratory for the larger world. We may learn and practice our vocations within the church, but our focus is meant to be the whole world. Maybe that's also why we try to box up transformative leadership in tidy packages, neatly tied about with vows and collars. Jesus wasn't so interested in such things. Nor were the great leaders among the saints.

Some of you may know the name of Roland Allen, who was a missionary in China in the late nineteenth century. He took Paul's line in terms of evangelism, and insisted that the job of a missionary was to give the scriptures and the sacraments, and then get out of the way. Sure, he'd go back and check in periodically, but he understood that most of the work was sowing the necessary seeds. I had the great privilege to go to China last fall, and see some of the fruit of his work. I saw two different aspects—Bishop Ting, at ninety-three the last of the old Anglican bishops in China, who at mid-life began to let go of a lot of the structural trappings of the kind of Christianity that had formed him. I also got to meet the leaders of the Three Self Patriotic Movement, which is what post-denominational Christianity is called in China today. The TSPM is thriving and growing so fast that it's stretching the government's attempts to keep tabs on it. It comes in lots of different liturgical and theological flavors, but it's remembered the Christian charism of oneness. And it's remembered what Roland Allen taught them, what he learned from Paul—that a local church should be self-sustaining, self-governing, and self-propagating. Those are the three "selfs" of the TSPM. Most leaders I spoke with didn't recognize the name of Roland Allen, but what he taught them clearly took root.

Those concepts are also what have historically underlain Anglican mission, and they underlie the movements today toward a baptismal understanding of ministry and leadership. In different places it's called total common ministry, team ministry, or ministry of all the baptized. Wayne Schwab has written an excellent book about teaching and equipping the baptized for this kind of leadership, *When the Members Are the Missionaries.*

This is an incarnational understanding of leadership—it's Pauline, and depends on discerning the gifts people have been given in discerning their vocation. It's not top-down—it requires a flatter understanding of shared authority in the Body. Theologies of leadership that look to the cleric as another Christ often have trouble with this. But baptismal leadership depends on a theology of each person being the image of Christ, the image of God. It takes the work of the spirit seriously, and insists that the spirit is still working—the work wasn't all finished at sundown on Pentecost. It also expects new forms in the Body of Christ, for we truly are a church always reforming itself. As that old hymn puts it:

New occasions teach new duties, time makes ancient good uncouth,
They must upward still and onward, who would keep abreast of truth.[10]

Yes, there are challenges in moving from an "expert" or Gnostic model of leadership to a discovery and discernment model. There are a host of associated challenges: moving from directive to collaborative leadership; from leadership focused on the institution (as fixed and defined) to a system that is networked, organic, and evolving; from closed and final revelation to continuing revelation. There are associated issues of power, particularly in how power is related to responsibility, authority, oversight, and servanthood. But if we start with a servant leadership model, then power struggles can be named and examined, and power can be used more constructively in service to the gospel.

In particular, there are signs of an emerging theology of episcope as shared ministry, which draws heavily on the body theology of Paul. David Moxon, Bishop of Waikato and one of the co-primates in New Zealand, has written a paper on shared episcope and its relationship to total, common, shared ministry. He began to wrestle with it from the sense that his context demanded something different—geography, particularly large geography, can be a motivational blessing to theological inquiry! So can leanness and shrinking financial resources. A lot of our structure as the Church of Christendom grew up in a culture of unquestioned luxury. But there is much to be learned in the desert, and the church's entry into a post-Christendom desert in this hemisphere is also filled with blessings—subtle ones, which we have to search for.

Conversations about other understandings of episcopal ministry ask questions that may be challenging for some. What about a bishop who also serves as rector of a congregation? Why not? That is, after all, the ancient understanding of the bishop in the center of the city, from which we grew the concept of the metropolitan. What about area bishops who serve particular geographic regions of the same diocese? That's a novelty in the American context, but it exists fruitfully in Australia and in Canada. What about episcopal systems or teams, which use the council and counsel of the clergy? If the bishop is understood to be chief missionary, then the episcopal task is to explore all possible missionary strategies. It should be obvious that this is not all new thinking. Even the Celtic models of monasteries have something to teach us and ways to provoke our thinking: double monasteries with abbesses or abbots as communities of discernment, equippers for ministry in the local community, and equippers and motivators of missionary voyagers, off to share good news with enemy raiders. What would the Celtic voyager look like today? Sending a small group of young people off on their bicycles to listen to and tell God-stories in the pubs of Denmark or the Netherlands?

Yes, there are various understandings and perspectives about leadership around the Anglican Communion. As long as we don't have to live with just one, there is abundant possibility for creative encounter with the spirit's leading. Our biggest trap right now is the tendency to think we can answer these questions for all time. If we think the spirit is still speaking, then we must assume there's more to learn, and good reason to keep asking questions.

Let's look more specifically at something your organizers asked me to address: the qualities, skills, experience, and training needed for women to thrive as leaders. If we take the body theology seriously, then we have to understand that lots of different gifts can be put to work in episcopal leadership. I don't think there's any magic inoculation for this work. I believe there are a number of what we might call virtues, or habits of character, that will bless the work of leadership, wherever and however it is expressed. At their deepest level, these are about the shape of one's spirit and the size of one's heart.

- *Courage and the willingness to risk.* Courage comes from a deep confidence in being beloved of God, in knowing that nothing can separate us from that love, including death, failure, social opprobrium, or the ecclesiastical equivalent of being labeled a feminist, a bitch, or even nastier things. Being wise as serpents and innocent as doves means using the gifts you have, in all humility, and not worrying too much about the consequences. That's what got Dom Helder Camara labeled a communist; it's what got Jesus executed. And both their words and spirits are still at work. The world won't be healed without what poet Toni Cade Bambara calls "sheer holy boldness." It's the kind of rich and pervasive sense that we're going forward whatever gets lobbed our way, because we're following where we've been asked to go—not unlike the widow who keeps pounding on the judge's door, year after year. Crazy old lady? So what? Her persistence worked! It also worked for the women who stood every day for years in the public square in Argentina, until their "disappeared" loved ones were noticed. The first day was the hardest. It gets easier with practice.

- *Creativity and playfulness.* That courage is renewed by connection to our created nature. I'd call that connection creativity and playfulness, reflecting the reality that we're all different, even though we're all made of the same basic stuff. Some have said that creation is merely—or mostly—God at play. That's also where humility comes from—being connected at a basic level with the dirt, the humus, the organic fertilizer that helps to make things grow and makes us human. If you can't laugh at the thought that you, your lover, and your enemy are all made out of that same stuff, well, God still has work to do with all of us. A sense of humor is essential, and despite the similarity of the words, "human" comes from "humus," and "humor" comes from "water." The dust from which we are made and to which we return is enlivened by the moist breath of God. And baptism has something to do with that, too.

- *Interconnection* is a theme that runs through all of this—knowing ourselves part of a larger whole. It's the basic religious response, and when we begin to turn our hearts over to that larger-than-me understanding, a radical sense of compassion begins to flourish.

- *Compassion* can get you moving when courage initially quails. Compassion is also rooted in that ability to dream the dream of more with God.

- *Dreams are essential.* A leader can't lead without a sense of direction. Until we can begin to share a part of the mind and heart of God—they are the same in Hebrew understanding—we don't have an effective goal or direction or even the beginnings of a map. But that big dream has to be continually revisited, re-examined in the face of the particularities of human existence. We don't live there all the time, but we have to continually point to it, like John the Baptist did.

- *Curiosity and hope.* Hope because we must have an assurance that our big dream is possible, even in part, in this life. Hope because there will be long years of seemingly no progress, and heart-wrenching situations that seem to invite the conclusion that God is absent. And hope because that's often all we have to give the people we're leading. It's related to curiosity because if we take the picture of how things are now and what the great dream of God says they should look like, we may have hope, but we don't have any ability to move from here to there without asking questions, trying unexpected approaches, and meeting odd people. Curiosity keeps us looking for the spirit at work and affirms our belief in the remarkable abundance of the love of God, who's had a hand in creating all this glorious mess!

So maybe that's a tall order, but that's what leadership needs. The *good* news is that none of us exhibits all these habits of the heart perfectly all the time, *and* that we have a community who is in this with us. The good news is also that we can hone these habits of the heart with practice—as in "practicing our faith."

I'll sum up those habits as: courage and risk; creativity and playfulness; interconnection and compassion; curiosity and hope; dreams and the big picture.

What must happen so that women can exercise the gifts each has been uniquely given rather than modeling themselves on others? I am convinced that when we take Pauline body theology seriously, we will set free all categories of human beings for leadership that accords with their gifts. We have the *confidence* that we are here to give glory to God, and to grow up into the full-ness of Christ. If you'll pardon my French, to hell with "roles"—we're not here to play roles, and it is literally to be in hell to live in a way that is not conso-nant with our God-given gifts. Christian leadership is about holy living and transformation, not filling someone else's expectations for how we should act, dress, speak, or lead.

I'll be pragmatic for a minute. Some have pointed to the disjuncture within our processes of discernment for ordained leadership. We understand that indi-viduals may have a personal sense of vocation to be a priest. We understand that some are called to be deacons. But virtually no one will admit to a sense of voca-tion as a bishop until after election—or appointment. I'm not going to say what some of you expect. It took a lot of convincing for me to admit the possibility of any of those vocations, and the vocation in which I am now serving. My experi-ence is of discernment in community leading the process, and of having to listen to others tell me I needed to listen. I'm not so stupid that I didn't learn to pay attention a little sooner each time, but I have not lived with the personal sense of call that I have heard many of my brothers and some of my sisters discuss.

At least in some dioceses of the Episcopal Church, we are beginning to live into a model of discernment that insists the community is essential from the very beginnings of the process—for *any* kind of vocation. The really intriguing things going on have to do with groups, not unlike Quaker clearness commit-tees, who will sit with a teenager wrestling with educational direction, or a new retiree trying to figure out what the next chapter of life is going to address. But those of us in ordained ministry still live with a great mixed-up mess that says both kinds of discernment, personal and communal, are essential, but doesn't say much about what that looks like. Different communities work it out in fear and trembling. The most important thing it says about the question we're here to talk about is that we have to do a better job of discerning gifts for epis-copal leadership in our peers and colleagues, and encouraging people to take the risk of exploring that possibility in community. No discernment work is ever wasted, whatever the proximate conclusion may be. We need to invite our fellow members of the body into discernment with appropriate humility and pride about our gifts and theirs. Note the now-stock distinction between what is traditionally understood as masculine sin (excessive pride) and feminine sin (inadequate pride). We can do a better job of teaching the church about that.

I want to say one other thing that I've learned out of my own experience, and the experience of other bishops whom I know well. We learn most of the technical stuff on the job. Put another way, there is an ontological change to the ordination and consecration of bishop—the gifts needed are usually given, and often employed. Being a parish priest is a vastly different vocation than being a bishop. The commonalities have to do with the spiritual habits I've tried to spell out in the last few minutes. That said, there is a great opportunity for formation, education, and training in the early months and years of episcopal leadership. Our House of Bishops has adopted a three-year plan that includes coaching from a bishop who has a few more years in office (but not too many!), an annual week-long opportunity for education and fellowship, and ongoing continuing education for the entire House when it gathers. That represents a significant change in the last ten years, and we function quite differently as a result. Most of us think this consciousness has brought a greater depth to our relationships and increased health to the way we work together.

What would I say to you in the Church of England? Do not lose heart, for God is in the midst of this long process. In the meantime, just go do it: serve the people, feed the sheep, start congregations, change the world. There is no stopping the good news of a people set free. There's a piece of me that wants to leave you with the courage to try the Benedictine solution: "It's far better to ask forgiveness than to get permission." Don't let an oppressive atmosphere stop your creative ministry. If it is of God it will prosper.

And do what you can to encourage and foster your own leadership and that of *all* the members of this church. After all, a change in the grass roots can change the fruit at the top of the stalk. How to grow that leadership ability and capacity? Tend the body—your own, and your community's. Seek health, wholeness, holiness in body, mind, and soul; seek it in sabbath-keeping and rule of life. Keep on learning, seek to be better equipped, ask for constructive criticism. That is where confidence is born and nurtured. Tend the flock of your own community, for we are not saved as individuals. When the body is healthy, all the members are. Look for those on the outside—this shifting paradigm offends some who want a purely personal savior, and the agitation of those on the outside can keep the body from being whole. Build and nurture connections, even unlikely ones—God, after all, is at work in places beyond our imagining. Welcome and practice creativity, tend to the vision, learn courage, maybe starting with physical courage. And remember that truth-telling in a world that does not want to embrace too much light can be hazardous, but it is the road to Easter.

We've wrestled a great deal here with the dream of God that drives Christian leaders to foment change toward that ideal. I want to leave you with a bit of etymology. That word "dream" has two old senses in English, which probably come from different roots. One means "joy, mirth, music," and the other is the kind of experience Jacob and Joseph had in the middle of the night. There's something about the dream of God that embraces both the merry celebration and the subconscious visitation. When the dream of God becomes real, there is indeed great cause for rejoicing. And when we all finally awaken in the dream of God, there will be no more separation between sleeping and waking, for we will all see God face to face, and there will be no more weeping or sorrowing.

May God continue to bless your ministries of leadership. Joy and dreams!

Waiting for the Prince of Peace

Jerusalem, Israel
St. George's Cathedral
Palm Sunday, 10:30 a.m.

16 March 2008

I had the great privilege to visit the Diocese of Jerusalem during Holy Week. This diocese does not yet ordain women, though the bishop is working toward that end. The congregation usually has many visitors, of different Christian traditions, as well as a vibrant Arabic and English speaking community in East Jerusalem.

Matthew (26:36–75) 27:1–54 (55–66)

Early Friday morning I went out for a run in New York City. A mile or so out, I started seeing police officers, little groups at first, all walking in the same direction. Soon I came upon a gathering of a couple hundred of them, standing on a street corner, stretched out half a block in each direction. I had no idea what was going on. I kept going, and on my way back half an hour later, I discovered the same group, just beginning to disperse. I made my way through them, and suddenly I heard, "Bishop!" I don't get recognized on the street very often, especially in my running clothes, but a young officer ran up, told me his name, said he was the clergy liaison officer for the NYPD, and that he wanted an appointment. I said I'd be happy to see him, and we both went on our way.

When I left the office that afternoon, the driver told me we'd have to take a different route to the airport. The president was in town, and that was the reason for the big gathering of police—they'd been getting their instructions. When George Bush comes to town, the police come out to pave the way, to make sure the streets are free from obstructions and the dissenters are kept at bay. The police line the street to prevent violence—and our president, whoever he is, seems to generate a lot of violent opposition. It seems to be true of most government leaders—witness the number of assassination attempts on recent presidents around the world.

Today we remember the arrival of another head of state. King Herod used to have a similar kind of armed guard when he came to Jerusalem at Passover. But when King Jesus comes to town, no police or soldiers line the streets—there are only people ready and eager for a different ruler. Crowds clamor, hoping for a kingdom of justice, praising God, looking for an end to oppression. This is no military leader riding a tank, no political despot in an armored limousine. Jesus comes openly, undefended, and the crowds respond by lining his path with branches of palm. That palm is called "phoenix" in Greek, a name that also points to the radical change of death and resurrection. Truly a different ruler is coming, promising radical and abundant change—the kind of change that prophets have taught us to seek for thousands of years.

What contrast between one who seeks and needs protection, and one who comes undefended! What contrast between the powers of this world, clamoring for an unchanging status quo, and the powers from above that urge change toward that divine vision of shalom and salaam.

For this prince of peace will bring a kingdom that transcends earthly grasping, whether of power, wealth, or geopolitical control. This Lord will claim God as *abba*, known more intimately than any earthly parent, rather than one to be obeyed out of fear. This mighty counselor will offer divine wisdom, learned in loving God, so that we might love and serve, rather than exploit, our neighbor.

In this land called holy, we still wait for that prince of peace. We still seek a Lord who will work a reconciled peace with justice, here and around the globe. No wonder that when Jesus entered Jerusalem, the whole town was in turmoil. Who is this prophet? Who is this man who promises another kind of kingdom, another realm where there will be no hungry or sick or imprisoned ones, where none will be unemployed, where none will be segregated from their neighbors and treated with a different justice because of their ethnicity or their religion?

The turmoil Jesus stirred up ended in his execution as an enemy of the state. Prophets tend to do that—stir things up and end up dead. That is part of the invitation Jesus offers each of us: to pick up our cross, to die to self, to proclaim the word of God in Jesus, to dream that divine dream of peace, and to be willing to die to everything else. We're invited to stir things up, for this world hasn't yet reached that divine dream of shalom. We're invited to recognize that death will be involved. There is no possibility of new life, of resurrection, without death. We will never know a healed world unless the systems that depend on violence or armed guards to maintain them die.

Jesus went unprotected—without the comfort of a family at home, without armed guards, without a place to lay his head, without a big political organization to back him up. He went simply, clothed in the spirit, protected by the anti-weapon of a palm branch, and welcomed by the poorest of peasants.

Out of that weakness and humility were death and despair extinguished. Out of the emptiness of human flesh, the same flesh as the debt-slaves and displaced people around him, God restored hope.

We share the great hope of Jesus the anointed one, because we are made of the same mortal flesh, and we, too, have been anointed to preach peace to the poor and deliverance to the captives. We died with Jesus in the waters of baptism, and we rise with him as well. We have been invited into this journey with him—this blood-red and passionate journey of sacrifice, of making-holy this still unhealed world. This road into the eternal city of peace leads past the cross. It includes turmoil and threat, but it is meant to be answered by the methods of peace—palm branches, donkeys, truth-telling, and the unexpected wind of the spirit.

That unexpected wind answers the world's violence with non-violence, with humor, and gospel overturning, by inviting the world's outcasts into the center of the circle, by the absurdity of a leader of state riding a donkey. Jesus' peace parade meets the performance violence of suicide bombs by building hospitals and schools for all the children of Abraham. We can become actors of non-violence with the phoenix branches of love. We can work reconciliation with the strangest of people—those of other faiths, and even police officers who seek out clergy. That is the dream of Yerushalayim. That is the dream of God, born in Jesus, dead and buried and raised again, prince of peace.

Hosannah in the highest. Blessed is the one who comes in the name of the Lord, the Lord of heaven and earth.

PART THREE

COMMUNION AND CONNECTION

The Image of God

New York, New York, USA
28 February 2007

This was webcast a couple of weeks after a meeting of the Primates of the Anglican Communion, the official communiqué from which had produced considerable anxiety in the Episcopal Church. It was broadcast from Trinity Church, Wall Street.

Good morning to all of you. And it is a good morning—as the psalmist says, "This is the day the Lord has made. Let us rejoice and be glad in it." Let us rejoice and be glad in the good and creative ministry going on in so many parts of this church and around the world. That is indeed an enormous blessing in a broken and hurting world.

I am grateful for this opportunity to speak to and with you, and grateful to Trinity Church for making this format possible. I'm going to review what has happened at the recent meeting of the primates, and offer a perspective that we might bring to the current situation. The last portion of this webcast will be devoted to a question and answer session.

The recent meeting of the primates in Tanzania included fourteen new primates, representing over one-third of the leaders of the provinces of the Anglican Communion. Several longer-serving primates are due to retire in the next couple of years, all of which is a reminder that change is a constant, including in the structures and leadership of the Anglican Communion.

The very structure of the meeting represented a change, too—in a break from tradition, three other bishops of our church were invited to address a session early in the meeting. What the primates heard from those three, and from me, was intended to give a broader picture of the circumstances in the Episcopal Church in America, represented in some quarters as dire. They heard the pain and anger of those in the minority in this church, who feel that their understanding of biblical morality is undermined by recent developments around human sexuality. The primates also heard that the bulk of our church, and our ecumenical partners, do not see these issues as centrally important to our understanding of salvation and the gospel.

The majority of this church is willing to live with the current state of our conversation in regard to human sexuality, or to continue to move ahead in recognizing the full and equal dignity of gay and lesbian Christians, and the appropriateness of their serving in all orders of ministry in this church.

That position, however, is a distinct minority within the Communion. The primates themselves represent a broad diversity of opinion. In all the conversations that ensue, it will be helpful to remember that while a primate may be the leader of his province, that province also has a diversity of opinion. That diversity is becoming increasingly evident in this Internet age.

A number of the primates represent provinces, especially in westernized or developed nations, where homosexuality is recognized and discussed. Some of those provinces are, or are soon likely to be, faced with the issue of civil unions and the church's attitude toward them. Those primates may agree or disagree with the Episcopal Church's recent actions in consecrating a bishop who is in a committed same-sex partnership, but they understand that those decisions are not sufficiently important to break communion.

There is another group of primates whose provinces are not generally discussing these issues in any major way, and who are frustrated by the level of energy focused on them. Issues of poverty and disease, and the other issues represented by the Millennium Development Goals, are far higher on their agendas. Generally, they do not see our church's actions as rising to the level of breaking communion, either.

There is a final group of primates who are exceedingly exercised about the Episcopal Church's actions, and see them as anti-scriptural and incredibly difficult as they attempt to evangelize in their own contexts. It is those primates, or bishops in their provinces, who have entered congregations and dioceses here in the United States, to offer oversight and episcopal ministry, generally uninvited by the local Episcopal bishop. Those primates and bishops who are crossing into this church report that their actions have been taken out of concern for the pastoral care and well-being of people in congregations here. Whatever you may think about the actions of those bishops and primates, it behooves us as Christians to assume that they have acted in good faith until we are confronted by evidence to the contrary.

Those bishops are seeking to offer pastoral care to the minority among us in the United States who disagree vehemently with the direction and decisions of recent General Conventions regarding human sexuality. That disagreement in some instances goes back many years, to the adoption of a new prayer book and the decision to ordain women to all orders of ministry, and those earlier disagreements may underlie the current difficulties.

Those disagreements, and the way they are increasingly being played out on a global stage, are responsible for what you have seen in the communiqué from this recent meeting of the primates. We Anglicans are being encouraged to find a way to work out our differences, or at least find a way to manage them, through actions within the Episcopal Church here in the United States. We have been asked to clarify some of our actions at General Convention, and to find a way to provide pastoral care for our dissenting minority.

The details of those requests are in turn generating considerable anxiety within our own church. The majority of American Episcopalians, as represented by General Convention's decisions, are being asked to pause in their journey toward the full recognition of same-sex partnerships as an equally appropriate and holy manner of life for Christians, in the same way that marriage or celibacy have long been recognized to be. We are asked not to consent to the election of partnered gay or lesbian priests as bishops, and we are asked not to authorize public rites for the blessing of same-sex unions. Both issues are addressed in the Windsor Report, and both were addressed by resolutions of the last General Convention. Some among the primates were dissatisfied with the responses we made at our convention last summer, despite the recognition of a group charged with assessing our answers, which indicated a belief that we had made a good-faith response, to the degree that we were able.

The primates have also made a further request of us. They have asked us to establish an alternative way to provide pastoral care to our dissenting minority—a variation on a proposal that a group of bishops and I made last fall. This proposal would have us provide pastoral care to dissenting Episcopal parishes or dioceses through bishops of our own church rather than bishops from other provinces in the Anglican Communion. A Pastoral Council would oversee this proposal, both from the perspective of our own dissenting minority and to ensure that overseas bishops withdraw from interventions within our church. We are asked to indicate our response to these requests by the end of September.

That time frame is not the only one with which we are contending. A larger project is under way to seek an Anglican Covenant. This is an attempt to develop a statement of what we believe about our common fellowship as Anglicans in communion with each other, and the interdependent nature of those relationships, including limits on the autonomy of the member churches, and those attending the primates' meeting received an initial draft of such a covenant. That draft is open to discussion and critique in the coming months. There is hope for a revised version before the Lambeth conference in the summer of 2008, and a further revision following Lambeth, at which time the Covenant may go to the various provinces for consideration, in particular to our General Convention in 2009. The expectation of a larger framework like the proposed Covenant, within which Anglicans can wrestle with difference, gives us a more reasonable time frame for clarifying how and where we want to stand as a church, and would permit General Convention to speak on the current issues.

While the current controversy has much to do with varying understandings of scriptural authority, there is also an element that has to do with a changing understanding of who may exercise authority. Our polity and our liturgy as a church insist that the voices of all the baptized are essential, and that all have equal dignity in the deliberations of this church. Recent actions of our General Convention have said that gender and sexual orientation are immaterial to the exercise of ordained ministry, and all of that is a challenge to some in this Communion. Actions by the primates at their last two meetings, and the actions of some of those primates in our province, also represent a challenge to the polity of the Anglican Communion, particularly over whether primates or the Anglican Consultative Council have the right and responsibility to exercise the kind of authority reflected in the current communiqué. The requests of the two most recent communiqués flow out of an understanding that bishops in general, and primates in particular, exercise a ministry of administering and overseeing the teaching of our faith. The current controversy is understood to represent a challenge to the generally accepted teaching of the Communion.

The greatest challenge in all of this is the inability of many to live with the tension that these developments represent. Anglicanism has traditionally been comfortable with, or at least willing to put up with, a significant diversity of theological opinion and a range of practice. The system we call the Anglican Communion is at present seemingly unable or unwilling to live with that kind of diversity. Parts of our own church are in a similar situation. Some see our current situation as rooted in competing values—either a justice that seeks the full inclusion of all, particularly sexual minorities, or an appeal to a traditional understanding of sexual ethics. Yet there are aspects of the current situation that cry out for a broader understanding on all sides, which call us to see that different viewpoints represent not competing but complementary Christian values. An ethic of justice and inclusion would seemingly also urge us to include the dissenter. A traditional understanding of sexual ethics has a great deal to say about fidelity and monogamy and relatively little to say about the gender or reproductive status of the partners.

We are being pushed toward a decision by impatient forces within and outside this church who hunger for clarity. That hunger for clarity at all costs is an anxious response to discomfort in the face of change, which characterizes all of life. On the Sunday before Lent began, we heard an account of the transfiguration. Jesus goes up the mountain with a few disciples, and they see him revealed in all his glory. The disciples try to fix that experience by building tents that will permit them to remain where they are. Then a cloud comes over them, and they hear the voice of God saying, "This is my beloved; listen to him." They don't stay in their little structures, and they don't remain in the cloud. Jesus urges them back onto the road, to follow where he leads.

We are struggling over the direction of that journey. The impatience we are now experiencing is an idol, a false hope that is unwilling to wait on God for clarity, an idol that fails to hope and expect that the Spirit will lead us into all truth. The biblical response to that kind of anxiety is always the message of the angel who says, "Fear not. Be not afraid, for God is with you." God is with us, and will continue to be with us, whatever this church decides. God will continue to be God, and God will continue to be worshiped in our churches, and God will continue to be served in our mission and ministry in this church and abroad.

Much has been said about the listening process urged by the last three Lambeth Conferences. There is some good news in that department. Conversations have begun in many places across the Communion, even in some of the places where primates are most neuralgic about these issues. Ten years ago, many of those primates were able to say with impunity that there were no gay or lesbian people in their dioceses or provinces. It is no longer possible to make that assertion. I would like to encourage us as a church to consider how we ourselves might listen more carefully to those with whom we most vehemently disagree. Can we, in a focused way, pay attention to the grief and suffering, and the love for God and neighbor, in those in other places on the theological and rhetorical spectrum? If we gain nothing else from the coming months, that would be a great gift.

I have been in conversation already with the president of the House of Deputies about ways we can call the whole church to the kind of faithful listening that will be necessary before we make any decision. I expect initiatives to come from both the Executive Council and from the House of Bishops that will invite us into deeper discussion of the possibilities this challenge presents. You will hear more from your bishop and from your deputies to General Convention in the coming weeks, and I hope you will participate when the opportunity comes.

If we can lower the emotional reactivity in the midst of this current controversy we just might be able to find a way to live together. That was the genius behind the Elizabethan Settlement back in 1559, which established the "middle way" so valued by Anglicans in the years since. Now more than ever we need to find a middle way through this controversy. A restrained and gracious response to this situation will need space and time to operate, and perhaps an unexpected or even humorous response. While these issues are of major importance, it is our very intensity about them that is preventing a life-giving resolution.

As we journey through this Lenten experience, I encourage you to reflect on Jesus' experience in the Garden of Gethsemane. He asks the disciples to watch and wait with him as he approaches his hour of judgment. We, too, are asked to watch and wait in this hour. Judgment will come in God's time, not ours. In the meantime, we can stay awake and be aware, and we can pray. Our task is not to run from this trial, but to continue to do God's work and to listen for the still, small voice saying, "Fear not. You are my beloved."

Finally, as Lent continues, I ask you to continue to fast from ascribing motives to others, to seek Christ in the stranger, and to ask God to quiet your fears. May we continue to work and pray for those who die daily from hunger, lack of medical care, war, and oppression. Pray especially for those who suffer because of their minority status, whether sexual or theological, for in Christ we are all a minority. And give thanks to God who has created us in all our variety. As frustrating and annoying as that variety may be, it is the image of God.

Religion and Science

Corvallis, Oregon, USA
Oregon State University
19 April 2007

This address was given to a group of OSU students and faculty, as well as members of the larger community. The group included old friends as well as strangers, and included many for whom this has been an ongoing conversation for years.

When I first rolled into Corvallis as a twenty-year-old graduate student, I had no idea what the future might bring. This institution and community have nurtured me both as a scientist and as a person of faith, and I am doubly humbled to stand here tonight.

We're here to talk about science and religion, and the challenge and possibility of their interaction. We live in a world that has in recent years either seen the two spheres of knowledge as fundamentally opposed, with relatively little to say to each other, or has uncritically assumed them to be interchangeable or to provide identical conclusions. It has been rare to insist that each is a valid way of seeking to know the world, and that indeed each has much to offer the other in complementarity (how each complements the other) and expansiveness (how each adds to the understanding the other can offer) in the human endeavor. I would further suggest that neither of those first two approaches—mutually exclusive or fuzzily identical—is honest to the best of either science or faith.

Science and faith are both ways of seeing the world around us—lenses, worldviews, or interpretive schemes for interacting with what is. They both seek knowledge and understanding of the world. Science at its root means "knowing," and in the Middle Ages, theology—the study of God or divinity—was known as the queen of the sciences.

Science seeks to know and understand the world of physically observable phenomena. It tends to ask questions about what is going on, how a phenomenon has arisen, and what we might predict about the development of that phenomenon. It is the method or lens most of us choose when we want to know whether we're going to need a coat or an umbrella tomorrow—though in Oregon, that's hardly a question. Experience teaches that, except in July and August, you are far more likely to get wet than not, yet even that folk wisdom is based on the collection of a long series of observations in a crude statistical approach—that is, rain can be expected about three hundred days a year.

Science is a way of looking at the world that is willing to suspend judgment (and usually all value judgments) about what is seen—until a hypothesis is made, tested, and the data arising from that experiment can be evaluated against the original hypothesis. Science has traditionally been understood as a lens that can only cope with testable issues. The Enlightenment response has been to say, "If it can't be tested, it doesn't count," and its more secularist strands of thought have put religion in the same box (or dustbin). The Enlightenment response tends to say that matters of faith are not testable and therefore uninteresting.

Scientific ways of knowing underlie the technological advances that define the developed world today. Experimental methods have given us call centers in Mumbai that fill orders for telephone service in Corvallis. Experimental methods gave rise to cardiac catheterization and the ability to save the lives of people who would otherwise almost surely die. Experimental methods gave us nuclear weapons, and they have contributed to what are almost certainly rapidly increasing rates of climatic change. All of which is to say that science does not routinely ask questions about moral value. It is, at its foundations, amoral, not immoral.

Religion or faith can be substantially different things, but for initial purposes let's consider them together as one lens that looks at the relationship between human existence and the transcendent, or whatever is more than the individual or the here and now. Religion asks questions about meaning and relationship, like, "Why am I here?" and "How should I live?" The great and enduring religious traditions assert particular ways of being in the world, which are most often about how to be in relationship with both the transcendent and the immanent aspects of ultimate reality. Those great and enduring spiritual traditions also tend to assert that the transcendent can be experienced in some way in this life—or in other words, that there is a profound interconnection between the transcendent and the immanent.

Religion tends to be relatively uninterested in the mechanical "how" questions that science is so good at answering. If it answers such questions at all, it is in terms of meaning—this is where we came from, and what it means for our lives today and in the future. And that issue of meaning imposes values and judgments about right and wrong. Religion says, "If we are this kind of being, then this is how we should live." Religion, rather than suspending judgment about observations of the world around us, encourages them, because those values offer a framework that can encourage people to live in one way rather than another.

The transcendent is not often subject to the kind of hypothesizing and experimentation that is the basic diet of science, but it is open to a kind of experiential analysis—which may be why it's called "practicing a faith." Experiment is the foundation of that strand of religion called mysticism, and it is also the origin of moral theology, which is, after all, about custom and manner, what a society has developed over time as guidelines for living. William James' famous work, *Varieties of Religious Experience,* is a good example of a kind of observational or natural history approach to religious—and especially mystical—phenomena. At the same time, there is a pragmatic streak to most religious traditions that says that particular modes of being, or particular practices, which stand the test of time (that is, for which experimental data return positive and life-giving results) are the ones that should be followed. Over time, those experimental results come to be called "tradition." And while tradition is notoriously difficult to change, it does usually represent the codification of a value-positive result in an earlier age.

Let's go back to science for a minute. There are parts of science, particularly in areas that investigate very small and very large phenomena, in which practitioners have begun to sound as though they are speaking of the transcendent. The great passions of many eras in scientific inquiry, from the classical philosophers and their theories of four kinds of matter, to medieval alchemists, to the twentieth-century quest for a Theory of Everything or a Grand Unified Theory (take your pick—GUT or TOE), are all about a transcendent understanding of the origins and structure of the universe. Underneath that quest has often lain a quasi-religious attempt to "know the mind of God." At the very least, I think even the more secular among us would acknowledge that the passion behind that search is an expression of a desire to have knowledge of, or to understand, or to be in relationship with, all that is. Strict secularists and strict religionists would define the "all that is" in different language and with different concepts, but there is, in broad terms, a commonality to the quest.

All of which is to suggest that both science and religion have important things to say to all human endeavor, that they need not be understood as dealing with mutually exclusive areas of concern, and that at this stage in human history, we may not develop an adequate response to the dilemmas of existence without attention to both ways of knowing. Indeed, given current circumstances, we choose one without the other at our own, and humanity's, peril. Einstein put it neatly when he said, "Science without religion is lame; religion without science is blind."

Let's turn to the issue of authority and how authority functions in both religion and science. Authority has to do with recognition, significance, or the source of one's confidence. It also has to do with the ability to make decisions and take action, and the certainty that underlies that decision-making ability. The word derives from "author," and developmental theorists would encourage us to understand that in order to be most constructive, authority has to be acknowledged and internalized by an individual—it has to be self-authored. Authority can reside in individuals or systems. It can be the power attributed to force or it can be a gift from others. Consider the different kinds of authority ascribed to Martin Luther King, Jr., a police officer, the Constitution of the United States, or an invading army. We might variously characterize them as moral, legal, and forcible authority.

In the scientific system, authority resides in experimentally reproducible results. It begins with reason, a logical approach that follows a set and expected pattern of hypothesis, experiment, data analysis, and the revision of the initial hypothesis or the formation of a new one. That understanding of authority is the basic reason for peer-reviewed research, for the public reporting of research in journals, and for the "publish or perish" phenomenon—if you don't participate in the system by publishing, you have no authority. In practice, however, we know that scientists tend to ask questions and frame hypotheses in terms of received wisdom—what has come before and been shown to be adequate explanation for prior experimental results. That produces a certain aversion to new and wildly creative theorizing, or what Thomas Kuhn, who wrote extensively on the philosophy of science, called "scientific revolutions" or paradigm shifts. Even Einstein wasn't immune from this aversion—he really couldn't deal with the crazy kind of physics that Werner Heisenberg was dreaming up, and that limited his ability to think outside his own box.

There is a related phenomenon that involves the authority given to personal charisma—a halo effect, if you will. If a well-respected scientist holds a particular view, it's more difficult for junior scientists to get contrary results published. Something like that went on with Charles Darwin and Alfred Russell Wallace. The hometown boy got his news out first, and the outsider was largely forgotten, even though his data were at least as good. Generally, it takes a supermajority of evidence, from well-respected scientists, before a scientific community can receive a radically new theory and change its paradigmatic world view.

We could sum up that scientific understanding of authority as based on reason, respected writing, and another kind of authority that resides in tradition and the particular witness of certain eminent persons.

Religious traditions claim similar kinds of authority. Most begin by looking to sacred scripture, the bodies of writing that summarize, inspire, or codify various faiths—the Bhagavad Gita, the Pali Canon of Theravada Buddhism, the Koran, the Torah, or the Bible. Sacred texts may be oral as well as written, and the creation stories of many aboriginal traditions are a good example. Most often these writings tell the story of a charismatic, spiritually gifted individual, or the history of a people in relationship to the divine or transcendent. Sacred writings tend to show, by example or through a set of moral laws, how to live a good life. Enduring religious traditions, as that name implies, collect a set of practices and outlooks that embody that tradition. I spoke a bit earlier about the incorporation of reason and experience in those practices that become tradition. Almost all such religious traditions also hold up the witness of particular saints, holy people, exemplars, or the founders of their faith, who embody the values and principles of the tradition.

When we look at the sources of authority in science and religion, they are remarkably congruent:

- publicly known and respected writing (or the oral equivalent) that reports the experience of a group of people, and which has stood the test of time and experiment

- the experience of particular respected individuals, which becomes normative as a way of thinking or living

- tradition or received wisdom, defining "what we know to be true"

- reason and experience, as human beings both develop and validate all of the above

So why have religion and science found each other so threatening? It has something do with what each would critique within its own practitioners—we could call it either arrogance or sin, but it's basically the prejudice that only one way of looking at the world, one lens, is appropriate or adequate. In this era of human history, we can no longer ignore or repudiate any less-favored way of seeing the world, because each has important and even essential gifts to offer for the ultimate survival and flourishing of the planet and its inhabitants.

Let's begin to tackle this ultimate survival issue by talking about interconnectedness. If there is anything that science has been teaching us for the last hundred years, whether in physics, ecology, or chaos theory, it is that everything is connected to everything else. The particle physics experiment of reversing the spin of one of a remotely distant pair of subatomic particles yields the result that the other one changes its spin at the same moment. We are increasingly aware of the changes wrought on entire ecosystems by removing one species or radically reducing its numbers—whether sardines off the California coast or elephants in sub-Saharan Africa. Most of us have been exposed to the idea that small changes in ocean surface temperature in the tropical Pacific have significant and long-lasting effects on rainfall both here and in South America.

Interconnectedness is also a fundamental truth of most religious traditions—how I act affects both my neighbor and my relationship with the divine. In the tradition that I practice, that concept is most often expressed as an understanding that one person's salvation or well-being depends on the well-being of the whole community—or the entire global family. Individual exemption from the lives and suffering of others is impossible. It may be the great Western heresy to assert that an individual can experience salvation without the salvation of the whole community. That understanding of basic interconnection grows out of an earlier age's spiritual wisdom that insists that communities, not individuals, are the basic unit of real human existence.

We live in an age in which our connections to events and creatures across the globe are painted by the news media and our personal communications nearly every waking moment. We are increasingly aware that carbon outputs in developed regions and nations are having disproportionate effects on the lives of the poor in Bangladesh and the Solomon Islands. Science is showing us how this grand system works, and religion is beginning to say more loudly that we have a moral responsibility for those vast consequences of our behavior.

Interconnectedness applies to these two great realms of human knowing as well. Why might it be important for science and religion to talk to each other? We can all point to some of the disastrous results of the failure of scientists to communicate with people of faith—the school board wars over teaching evolution, the lack of popular understanding of that theory despite 150 years of teaching, and the lack of popular understanding about just what "theory" means. Religious scholars have a burden in the other direction. Consider, for example, the lack of understanding in many parts of the scientific community—as well in as popular culture—of the technical meaning of the word "myth" and its importance as a framework of meaning that can organize human communities through time. Myths are stories about a people's origins, not something patently untrue. Indeed, the popular misunderstandings of both "theory" and "myth" often insist that neither can possibly be true.

But the possibilities for fruitful conversation go far deeper, and theory and myth can inform one another. There are strands and pockets in both areas of inquiry that are beginning to find some common ground in talking about the nature of existence. I noted earlier the propensity of cosmology and the physics of the very small to speak in terms of mystery. The insights of chaos theory have moved vast areas of science beyond deterministic models, and that provides an opening to speak to religious scholars who hold an understanding of the divine that is neither mechanistic nor completely divorced from the observable.

The opportunity for real dialogue about the nature of the transcendent—and that may be a more fruitful term than God or the divine if it allows more scientists to participate—has not been this good for centuries. The Enlightenment brought a kind of stand-off in most cross-sphere conversation, as the transcendent was often used as an explanation for that which could not be understood in scientific terms—and that produced the old "God of the gaps" kind of rationalization, which provided few intellectually satisfactory answers. The transcendent, in religious terms, is almost always defined as being beyond full comprehension, as ineffable, unknowable, unnamable. That is not too far from the nascent realization in chaos science that the world is not fundamentally explainable or predictable. Many religious traditions understand the transcendent to be gracious—in some way inclined toward life and its flourishing rather than toward death and nothingness. Cosmologists speak about the remarkably narrow window within which the mathematical equations underlying our descriptions of the universe can function—the basic six constants are exceedingly finely tuned. The constants have to be within very narrow limits if the universe is to be stable enough to develop rather than explode or implode into nothingness. The balance between centripetal and centrifugal forces that allows stars to coalesce and planets to form is quite remarkable.

Theologians might speak about the transcendent in ways that accord with that understanding by using language and images such as "that which lures or encourages, imagines or dreams more existence or abundant life." Theistic traditions personalize that force, talking about God as love, the ground of being, or the process involved in free will. Hinduism speaks of human experience of the transcendent as "*tat tvam asi*—that thou art" and "*sat cit ananda*—being, consciousness, bliss." Buddhism seeks a path of transcendent enlightenment through relinquishing attachment and thus suffering. Other traditions speak of "the energy of life." Most spiritual traditions insist on some directionality to existence—that there is a goal or aim in life, understood spiritually. Theistic traditions often speak in terms of salvation; others may speak of release from the suffering of existence, or moving beyond the purely or largely corporeal realm. Most of those traditions address the fundamental human problem of suffering.

Scientists have no trouble engaging the idea of an emerging or evolving universe. The process of change, adaptation, and succession (though not always success!) is intrinsic to the scientific method. Theologians and people of faith are interested in, and variously committed to, existence in which suffering is eliminated or reduced. The cause of justice and peace has its roots in a profoundly religious imagination. Together, and in dialogue, these two spheres of human knowing have the possibility to accomplish parts of this vision in very pragmatic ways. I do not believe that either sphere—religious or scientific—can accomplish it alone.

How can an interaction between religion and science be fruitful? There is a strand of several traditions that has to do with prophetic critique. The prophetic voice, standing in a liminal relationship to the rest of the community or to the entire tradition, demands accountability from that tradition for not living up to its values. The prophetic voice also offers a vision or dream of what a religiously observant or value-based manner of life might look like. Most often these prophets have justice and compassion as their bedrock value and motivation. Society needs that kind of transcendent view in order to address its own lack of justice and compassion. Social systems, according to this strand of theologizing, are capable of profound evil, of denying the basic dignity of some parts—or the entirety—of human existence. Social systems, this strand of theology insists, can be guilty of working to diminish or even destroy some forms of human existence. In this framework, the cure—or the salvation—lies in right relationship to the divine and to the rest of creation.

The scientific enterprise is increasingly able to think and speak in similar terms. The destruction of ecosystems is the result of changes in relationships, too, both within and beyond the ecosystem, as species are pushed to extinction by changing climatic, predation, or pandemic factors. Paleontologists can describe myriad examples of these extinction events, and in some of the better understood systems, they can show how one ecological niche is repeatedly filled or exploited by successive species.

The theological enterprise, however, asks the moral question: when change is the result of human activity, is this the right thing for one species to do, encourage, or permit? And that leads us to the further question: should we see the human species in the same category as other species that have flourished for a time and then passed into fossil history, only to become latter-day curiosities? Both an overtly secular ethic and a religious one generally hold the value of human life in higher regard. The religiously motivated ethic also argues that the diminished lives of many, due to poverty, disease, malnutrition, or violence, are just as significant an issue as the ultimate continuation of the human species.

If we, as people seeking greater knowledge of whatever form, take our interconnectedness seriously, we must be concerned with the diminishment of human existence, with other forms of life, and with the rest of the universe. We may not yet know fully how the latest supernova will impact our individual lives, but most of us can be confident that the possibility is there, at least theoretically. We can be more certain that unrest in Zimbabwe, violence in Sudan and Nigeria, the rising drought in the American southwest, and even the health of spotted owls are both symptoms and causes worthy of our attention and concern, and that they impact people and communities far away.

The public service of community building—and I would argue that this is a higher good that can be embraced by people across the theological and scientific spectrum—requires knowledge of several kinds. Religious vision and knowledge—what is sometimes called enlightenment—can inspire people to dream dreams and think thoughts that lead them beyond narrow instinctual self-interest toward a healed world of peace and justice. That kind of knowledge may be ineffable, but it does create the passion, zeal, and energy that are required to struggle toward that vision. Religious or spiritual knowing says that the meaning of life has to do with right relationship to all that is. Scientific knowledge is essential both to understanding the technical and environmental aspects of human diminishment (such as those responsible for disease, global warming, and overexploitation of resources) and to developing effective technical responses. Science, however, cannot alone mobilize effective human responses, for we are not purely rational or mechanistic creatures.

If we fail to engage in this dialogue, we are likely to fail at the quests for both kinds of knowledge. The scientific quest to understand this global system will fail as it neglects to observe the participation of religiously motivated human beings, whether they have noble or ignoble ends in mind. Werner Heisenberg was right about more than physics when he postulated that the observer changes the observed—and this system called the human enterprise needs both critique and encouragement. The religious quest will fail if it neglects the pragmatic realities of our interconnectedness. Not only is the scientific method a potential arbiter of narrowly adversarial or competitive religious visions of reality, it is an important partner to the kind of spiritual knowing that is willing to dream beyond the mechanics of life toward equity, justice, and peace. Science is a way of understanding the workings of this world, whether at the level of quantum physics, ocean currents and weather systems, or the social dynamics of human beings in community. It is a way of knowing what we have to work with, and it can lead to testable hypotheses about the most effective means of changing what is.

Understanding the best of recent science is not a luxury. It is essential to building this vision of a healed, more whole, and healthy community—and I would point out that "whole" and "healthy" come from the same root as the word "holy." The human purpose, in its highest and loftiest conception, must be to heal this world.

Given the scientifically indisputable realities of global climate change, we would do well to remember the words of philosopher and poet Henri Frederic Amiel in the nineteenth century: "Life is short and we have never too much time to gladden the hearts of those who travel the dark journey with us. Oh be swift to love, make haste to be kind."

Gladdening hearts may seem a mild phrase, but the joy and possibility that is lost moment by moment is astounding. A billion people in this world lack access to clean water; 2.6 billion lack adequate sanitation. Two million children die every year as a result—one every fifteen seconds.

The clock is ticking. We are running out of time. Each moment we deny, delay, or obfuscate instead of responding effectively, we increase the likelihood of injustice to those who are the weakest, poorest, and least able to respond and adapt to the inevitable consequences of climate change. The people of Bangladesh, huddled by the millions on low-lying, flood-prone plains, have no refuge from storms of increasing intensity. The peoples of the South Pacific, within a few decades, are likely to lose their habitat to rising sea levels. We have seen that reality on our own Gulf Coast–it was the poorest who suffered the most from Hurricane Katrina. The people of Darfur are caught in a tightening spiral of desertification, in the midst of a whirlwind of increasing violence—and the two maelstroms are intimately connected. As we continue to expand our dependence on foreign oil, the people of the Niger Delta are increasingly living with air, water, and soil pollution from the extraction of oil—all of it accompanied by spiraling violence. We have the technical ability and capacity to vastly decrease our use of fossil fuels, and the accompanying carbon load on the atmosphere, but we have not yet found the moral and political will to do so.

Together, scientific wisdom and religious wisdom may be able to generate enough political will to respond. If we fail to build effective understanding and partnerships, neither sphere of human investigation is likely to have the long-term leisure to do much more on its own. Scientists can tell us with reasonable accuracy what is likely to happen to the physical world. People of faith are able to predict what is likely to happen to us all spiritually, and to insist on the moral responsibility we all share for making effective responses. A world of justice, shalom, and spiritual well-being— and our physical survival as beings of higher consciousness—depend not only on the ability of religion and science to talk to each other, but on our ability to build creative partnerships that can respond to the suffering of this world. To do less is to shirk our identity as people of higher consciousness, and to avoid becoming truly *human* beings.

Both science and religion lead people to see the world with enormous awe. The response can either be a burning desire to understand the workings of the physical world, or an equally burning desire to connect with whatever has brought this world into existence. Both kinds of passion can help us to care for this world and all its inhabitants, and both will be imperative if we are to relieve the suffering of many and bring increasing hope to our own species and all others.

Being an Episcopalian Tomorrow

Williamsburg, Virginia, USA
National Network of Episcopal Clergy
Associations NNECA—"Our Church Lives"

27 June 2007

This gathering happens regularly as an opportunity for clergy to network, learn, strat-egize, and advocate for issues directly related to their ministry in the Church. I was invited to speak to them about where I see this church going.

What does it mean to be an Episcopalian? Maybe that's a helpful place to start, especially if we want to think about what being one tomorrow might look like. Our church, especially in its relationship to the wider Anglican Communion, is caught up in a search for answers to that question, largely because our answers, and our church, are clearly changing.

What makes us Episcopalians? We might say using the Book of Common Prayer, having a church with bishops, or being in a historic relationship to the Church of England. But after all, the Methodists can make a lot of the same claims. I think there's something more essential that defines us as Episcopalians—our understanding of authority.

We claim three strands of inspired authority—Hooker's definition of scrip-ture, reason, and tradition. As Episcopalians, we also affirm the importance of a dispersed authority that's not vested in one particular prelate—or indeed in prelates alone. We share with other Anglicans an understanding of a church that is episcopally led and synodically governed, even though that looks very different in different parts of the Communion. Our history on these shores for more than two hundred years without the presence or leadership of bishops meant that the authority of the laity was being well developed here from the very beginning, and the voice and leadership of the baptized and of clergy other than bishops is both valued and energetically claimed.

That multifaceted understanding of authority leads toward a baptismal sense of authorization and ministerial empowerment—in very concrete terms, not just in the abstract. As we live into the theology of the 1979 Book of Common Prayer, Episcopalians increasingly understand that all the baptized—not just the ordained alone—participate in God's mission of healing the world, reconciling the world to God and one another in Christ. The members of National Network of Episcopal Clergy Association are here to talk about how the ordained lead, image, and encourage God's mission.

That Catechism definition of healing or reconciling the world does not specifically mention the rest of creation, although our awareness of interconnectedness today should encourage that. If we ever get around to revising the current prayer book, we will most assuredly be explicit about reconciliation including all creation.

This is what Jewish tradition calls *tikkun olam*—healing the world, and building a society of peace and justice summarized in the dream of shalom. Our understanding of our interconnectedness in the Body of Christ, and our interconnectedness to all of creation—which Sallie McFague calls the Body of God—means that none of us can live in fully right relationship with God or our neighbors if some of us are suffering, ill, in want, lonely, lost, or starving. Our care for the rest of creation is intimately bound up with the suffering of our human neighbors. And in similar ways, we are discovering new depths of what it means to be in communion with our fellow Anglicans around the globe.

I would like to hold up for you a framework for mission developed by the Anglican Consultative Council, called the Five Marks of Mission. They've been around for about twenty years, and they've been reinterpreted a couple of times, but they are little known in the Episcopal Church. They are a helpful summary of the elements of God's mission in which we participate, and despite their newness to many of us, that very difference may help to frame our conversation.

- *To proclaim the good news of the kingdom*: Here is Jesus' own mission statement in the Gospel of Luke: "The Spirit of the Lord is upon me, because he has anointed me to bring good news to the poor. He has sent me to proclaim release to the captives and recovery of sight to the blind, to let the oppressed go free, to proclaim the year of the Lord's favor." (4:18–19)

- *To teach, baptize and nurture new believers*: This is the Great Commission—for the sake of God's mission.

- *To respond to human need by loving service*: Faith without works, after all, is dead.

- *To seek to transform unjust structures of society*: We are to build a society of shalom.

- *To strive to safeguard the integrity of creation and sustain and renew the life of the earth*: We are to tend the garden.

The ministries of all the baptized, both lay and ordained, are shaped by those signs of mission. The ministry of deacons may have more traditionally been identified with the third, "to respond to human need by loving service," but deacons can and should provide leadership in all five of those areas. Presbyters have probably been most specifically identified with the second, "to teach, baptize, and nurture new believers," particularly presbyters in parish ministry. But I would encourage you to see that all of them are part of your ordained vocation. They are all about evangelical opportunities, and beautiful indeed are the feet of those who proclaim good news wherever they go.

If the ministry of the ordained is about modeling, encouraging, and equipping others for the ministry which all the baptized share, then I hope it's pretty obvious that a lot of our work is meant to be holding up this broad kind of understanding of God's mission, as well as working in partnership with all orders of ministry for the building up of God's kingdom.

As we look toward a third-millennium church and a renewed sense of mission, we might ask about new ways in which the ordained are likely to be called to serve.

Deacons could be sent out, asking, "Where is the good news going unheard?" "Who are the hungry in spirit, whose needs and concerns and hopes are not being addressed?" This is not a suggestion to divert energy from the physically hungry, the homeless, those in legal prisons, or any of the places in which deacons have traditionally worked to transform what is into something more like the reign of God. This is encouragement to think bigger.

What role might deacons and priests play in ministry to and with those who are captive to a consumerist society? Can you imagine a ministry toward people caught up in the rat race of jobs or shopping or keeping up with the neighbors? How about a ministry that calls forth gifts among our congregations' members— gifts that could lead toward forming communities of faith and transformation among co-workers or fellow commuters or soccer parents? That work would call on the community-organizing aspects of diaconal ministry and the gathering aspects of presbyteral ministry. All of it is about mobilizing the faithful to do and speak good news.

While most of us think we know and understand the ministry of presbyters, I encourage you to think about how that understanding and exercise of priestly ministry has been shaped both by the absence of deacons, and by the lack of full empowerment of lay ministry in many places. I yearn for a church in which presbyters are set free to exercise the central callings of their vocation. The ordinal of our church[11] is exceedingly clear about that vocation: it is "to proclaim by word and deed the Gospel of Jesus Christ," to serve all sorts of conditions of people in your care, to preach, and to participate in sacramental ministry. The possibilities of that vocation have most often been seen in parochial work, but I want to re-echo what I said about diaconal ministry. Where is the gospel going unheard? What are the openings and possibilities for spreading good news that you haven't yet explored?

It may be that deacons, at work in the world, are especially suited to say to the larger church, "Here is an opportunity to speak good news to a group of people that might result in building a faith community," and then challenging the structures of the church to respond. Much of our traditional understanding of church planting starts with the diocesan office studying community demographics—things like population, income, lifestyle, numbers of children, and ethnic composition. What if we asked deacons to tell us where the gospel is needed? The ministry of presbyters would be essential in nurturing those new communities, wherever they might be located—but deacons can tell us where they are.

We already know where some of those communities are. Consider *Prairie Home Companion*'s mythical Lake Wobegone. There's the Side-Track Tap and Norm's Pretty Good Grocery, the Chatterbox Café, or even Café Boeuf—all of which provide the seeds of a faith community not much different from the little communities who gather at Starbucks, in the company lunchroom, or on the morning bus or carpool. The anonymity of so many cities and suburbs today, with people locked in their walled homes, gated communities, and solo-occupant cars, speaks loudly about the need and hunger for intimate community. The church needs to move out into the community, and the people in this room have the ability and responsibility to facilitate that work. It may involve equipping members of congregations to go out and gather their fellow workers and travelers, or it may involve you yourselves going out into that hungry world.

I commend a book called *Take This Bread*[12] by Sara Miles, as an example of what church beyond church might look like. It's an exploration of a feeding ministry begun at St. Gregory of Nyssa in San Francisco that has spawned other sacramental feeding tables in the larger community.

The church in this millennium will often be less tied to buildings than it has been for hundreds of years. The research is telling us that younger generations are less interested in a spirituality of place than are people currently at midlife and beyond. The hunger of younger generations seems to be for a spirituality of practice—which sounds to me like an opportunity for the kinds of ministry you are gifted at and trained to do, both as deacons and as priests. How do we lead people hungry for good news into an awareness of the possibility of building shalom, so that the reign of God may be known in their own lives and the surrounding community? How do we begin to teach and nurture those searchers for kingdom-building work?

There is an important connection here that may not be obvious. I believe we need to be much more intentional about discerning, recruiting, forming, and sending ordained and lay leaders to minister to and with younger generations— and that means we need to begin to see those gifts in teenagers. You may know that the average age of an Episcopal cleric is fifty-seven. The average Episcopalian is roughly the same age. We may have a special vocation to minister with the aging, but that is not a ministry that can be replicated forever—it does not have an eternal future. I want to challenge all of you to look for leadership gifts among the younger folk around you. They may not have the maturity of a forty-year-old, but a fair number of you were ordained as twenty-somethings, and it appears that God has given you the gifts necessary to grow and mature in your ministry.

There are other, related opportunities for vocational discernment among the marginalized populations within and beyond this church. I firmly believe that those populations, and not the aging WASPs who are not replacing themselves, are the growing edge of this church. Our evangelical work must include a culture shift, however, in the same way that youth need to be seen as already possessing the gifts necessary for mission and ministry. Those populations have more often been seen as the object of ministry in this church, rather than its subject. The young, the poor, the marginalized can be—and indeed are—the actors and authors of ministry, not its passive recipients. I'll suggest another account of what that might look like—a book called *Call Me Child of God…Not "Those People"*, by Julia Dinsmore.[13] She talks about the gifts of the poor, and their capacity not just for survival—which is awesome—but their capacity for leadership. God has already blessed every one of us, and each community around us, with abundant gifts. But God has not always gifted the current leaders in the church with the perspicacity to see those gifts in unexpected places!

I came into this work of honoring and developing the gifts of all the baptized hearing about the work of Roland Allen, missionary in China in the late 1800s, who did evangelism and mission in the style of Paul. He saw his vocation as going into a community long enough to give the scriptures and the sacraments, and then getting out of the way. I firmly believe that we need to recover that sense of a church on the move, out in the world, rather than waiting for people to come through our lovely red doors. What about ministry among the incarcerated? I have met inmates who have gifts, both spiritual and practical, for mission and for ordained ministry. What about Hispanic ministry? Campus ministry? We as a church are not terribly good at setting people free to root the gospel in their own contexts; the institutional response to innovative ministry has more often been to root out the context.

We have so many norms and structures that seem essential to the way we've always done church. Consider this: Until recently, it has required a formal education, in residence, for three years, at a cost of a hundred thousand dollars, to gain the tools needed for sacramental ministry in a congregation. I am excited to tell you that the deans of our seminaries pretty clearly understand that that system does not work in all contexts and circumstances, and is likely to be less and less the norm. The deans themselves are beginning to have strategic conversations about how to provide education in ways that suit the new and changing contexts of this church. But the challenge goes far beyond education. It has to do with how we use the gifts we have—people, buildings, structures, tradition. We need to be eternally asking the question, "Are you being served?" with *you* being understood as the image of God. The answers may at times seem as nutty as that BBC farce, but if we are not asking the question, we're going to miss the Christ.

I wonder as well about the nature of full-time, full-stipend employment in one parish as the norm for presbyters in coming years. I think we're going to need all the well-educated ordained leaders we can produce, but I also believe that we're going to use them differently. Either they will serve significantly larger congregations, or they'll serve several congregations, or they'll work in the world as well as in the church.

I think we'll see a shift away from medium-sized congregations, at least ones who expect the full-time services of a priest. Congregations will have to be larger just to support the economics of a stipended cleric and staff. At the same time, if presbyters are set free to focus on their particular ministries, there is no reason why this should not be a creative response—but it will require deacons and an increasingly empowered laity. Those larger congregations, when healthy and vital, will have multiple smaller faith communities within them, places where people can be known in intimate community, where they can pastor and be pastored, and where they can learn, pray, and serve together. Those cell groups have a good deal in common with life in small congregations, of which I think we could see many more, if we are able to let go of that one (paid) priest, one parish idea. Smaller and rural communities already know some of the challenges and opportunities intrinsic in this shift, and they have something to teach the rest of the church.

There is a place as well for a new or recovered valuing of bi-vocational ministry. Those who labor in the world, whether lay or ordained, have access to situations in need of the gospel in ways that parish-based clergy seldom do.

Yes, we will have to die to old ways, but there is new life, and abundance, on the journey.

I expect we may see a shift in episcopal ministry in the next couple of decades as well. We already have economic situations in several dioceses that make it increasingly difficult to support the full-time ministry of a bishop. Can we envision a church in which some bishops are also functionally bi-vocational or bi-locational? Paul certainly managed to do it. We may even begin to broaden our understanding of episcopal ministry, seeing and valuing the oversight ministry of a leader who pastors a sizeable congregation as well as the surrounding region of a diocese, or who serves as ministry developer and bishop. Is that an area bishop, a suffragan, or something new? Jim Kelsey was working toward something like this in the Diocese of Northern Michigan, especially with his leadership team. This is likely to become reality sooner rather than later, and most likely it will be prompted by economic necessity. We need to be thinking now about the challenges and opportunities involved.

I can imagine increased ecumenical opportunity as well. We are already in full communion with the Lutherans, yet the on-the-ground realities are still profoundly separate in most parts of the two churches. We have begun interim Eucharistic sharing with the Methodists, but how many of us have even begun to explore that? The charism of mainline, critical Protestantism (one that invites rather than squelches inquiry) is not unique to any denomination, but it could grow and flourish in an environment of shorter silos. I firmly believe we have critical gifts to bring to the engagement of the gospel with post-modern society, and we will be far more effective if we can cooperate rather than compete.

In all of these creative possibilities, the challenge is to keep our focus on the mission opportunity. There will be enormous inertia that seeks to maintain old structures and particularities, but if we look back at our history, we'll see that resistance is more often a sign of death's finality than of resurrection.

Our identity as Episcopalians has to do with knowing who we are, whose we are, and what to do about it. Knowing ourselves beloved of God means we respond by engagement in God's mission of healing the world. We are gifted and authorized for that work by baptism, and some of us have been called to do that work in ordered ways.

All of it is about the glory of God, and if we remember Irenaeus' words about the glory of God being a human person fully alive, it is the way to abundant life.

A Climate of Change

Seattle, Washington, USA
Creating a Climate of Change: Renewing
the Earth through the Genesis Covenant

11 April 2008

*A portion of the closing event of a multi-day and multi-event conference, the final
celebration was at the Seattle sculpture park. This park is a physical witness to the
possibilities of re-creation, as it has involved redeveloping a toxic waste site. The
Genesis Covenant invites faith communities to reduce their carbon footprint by
50 percent in the next ten years.*

Create a climate of change—a tall order, but one that honors our fundamental
unity with all of creation. But change, of course, isn't always popular. In our tradition, we're fond of the story that asks how many Episcopalians it takes to change
a light bulb. "Change?" goes the response. "My grandmother gave that light bulb.
If it was good enough for her, it's good enough for me." Well, most of us know we
need to change that light bulb, and a good many more light bulbs as well.

Change is hard because part of our human condition is inertia—and that
inertia has contributed to our evolutionary success. Conserving tendencies
keeps us in known territory, doing familiar things. That has a lot to do with
how we learned which plants were good to eat and where and when the fish
could be caught.

But embracing appropriate change is also fundamental to our evolutionary
success. If we had never changed, we'd still be a bag of organic molecules—
probably not even protoplasm—in a sea much warmer than this one. Evolution,
whether the kind we think of when we invoke Darwin's name, or the kind that
comes to mind when we're talking about building a more just and peaceful human
society, depends on an appropriate balance between the sort of stationary, con-
servative inertia that lets us keep the best of what has come before us, and the
kind of dynamic inertia that keeps us exploring the new possibilities all around
us. We would be things, rather than living beings, without the capacity for both

innovative and conserving behavior. As Cardinal Newman said, to be human is to change, and to be perfect is to have changed often.

We are being urgently asked to create a climate of change, to encourage others, and ourselves, to look for those new possibilities, and to explore them with the courage to try the untested and unknown. The future is not a place for the faint-hearted.

But we're not called to embrace change without a sense of where we intend to go. That kind of unexamined behavior has brought us to this point of looming crisis. We're here today to encourage the kind of change that can offer a hopeful future for all of humanity and all of creation, so that all people may live an abundant life that does not do injustice to the rest of creation, and therefore to our neighbors. For we are all connected, and the actions of one part of this ecosystem—or the body of God, as one theologian calls it—ultimately affect all the other parts.

Renewing the earth will take significant and remarkable change. This conversation about reducing the carbon footprint of our structures is one part of a sweeping change of habit being urged on all of us. The conserving behavioral inertia of most human beings will only lead to a worsening future for all of us. This change of a variety of habits will call us to creative initiative like learning to modify the way we buy groceries—taking our own recyclable bags to the store, for example, and buying locally grown food when possible, and choosing products in minimal packaging, and eating lower on the food chain, and walking or biking to the store. That kind of behavior also has an impact on the carbon emissions from our buildings— we should be thinking about what it takes to erect the building, occupy it, and keep it operating.

The creative change that this covenant calls for is more challenging because a lot of it is not as obvious as getting food on the table. It is, however, just as urgent as eating three times a day, and if we don't begin to move in prophetic ways toward that goal, we will find both tasks increasingly difficult, if not impossible, within a few short years.

There are clear ways to change our greenhouse gas output—beginning with replacing incandescent bulbs with compact fluorescents, and turning down the heat in the winter. But some changes will be more challenging—like investing in wind or solar energy devices, insulating our buildings and improving their thermal inertia, calculating the optimal time lag for automatic light switches, adding green roofs and passive solar or earth-sheltered design elements.

We'll have to work as a community as well, to advocate for social policy that rewards green power generation rather than the old standard ways of producing power, especially by burning fossil fuel. That advocacy work must extend to new building codes that require green construction methods that produce rapid and effective results.

We'll have to carefully study the tradeoffs in new modes of energy production, like wave-generated energy and wind farms, and geothermal energy, like technologies that tap tidal energy and heat pumps that tap oceanic thermal structures. We didn't do a very good job of studying and providing for the consequences of the development of nuclear energy, and we're stuck with a very nasty pile of garbage as a result. Most of us, particularly the people of Nevada, are less than eager to put that waste away and forget about it.

In the technical and scientific communities there are hopeful developments around energy production, which must be balanced with care-filled ethical conversations prompted by religious communities. Will these new possibilities offer justice for all? Or will they unfairly burden some segments of the community? How are these possibilities likely to affect generations yet to come? What about the rest of creation? What are the costs of inaction in the face of uncertainties about those consequences?

Those of us who represent faith communities might consider how the use of our buildings could be improved. How many of those buildings sit empty most of the week? How might we share our physical resources with one another and with the rest of the community, for the benefit of the whole? Cutting our greenhouse gas output in half could almost be achieved simply by doubling up in our buildings! Putting the land on which those unoccupied buildings stand back into service as a green zone would almost certainly do it. Not unlike this park—or Gasworks, which not too long ago were toxic waste sites.

Creating a climate of change has deep roots in the prophetic strand of religion. Prophets are the folks who stand up, stick their necks out, and cry, "This world is a long way from the way God intended it to be. Shape up!" In other words, "Remember the dream, get with the program, and change." That kind of prophetic work is an act of imagination, for it remembers a deep truth, and it is a creative act of partnership with the creator who originally dreamed all this up and works to make that dream a reality.

Part of that prophetic work means imagining what seems unimaginable to our society. Giving up half of our buildings is an example, particularly in a culture that is obsessively focused on acquiring, consuming, and possessing. So is imagining other construction methods—a straw-bale temple?—and other uses. There are growing numbers of inner-city faith communities thinking about how they might build upwards, with one or more floors for worship and gathering, some for teaching (schools during the week as well as for teaching the faith), and more floors for low-income housing, maybe with a greenhouse on the roof. An Episcopal seminary in New York City is in the process of drilling geothermal wells around its property to provide heat-pump cooling and heating.

Faith traditions have a built-in way of encouraging and motivating change—that's why it's called "practicing the faith." It's about developing new habits so that we change the way we live on this earth and in relationship with those around us.

You and I, and the traditions we represent, are meant to be leaders in building a world that looks more like the divine dream for that world of peace and justice. We believe that dream means that people live in right relationship with God and all their neighbors, including the non-human parts of creation. Our task is to share that dream, teach people about it, and encourage them to participate in it. And given that we don't seem to have arrived at that dream just yet, it means change. Part of the prophetic work of recounting the dream is to engender a sense of urgency. We are blessed by the reality that growing numbers of people understand the urgency behind global climate change. Part of that work has already been done.

The partner of urgency is hope, and prophets know something of hope as well. We can give concrete examples of changed habits that contribute to achieving the dream—things like changing light bulbs and adding insulation, eating lower on the food chain and recycling bottles. We can show people how small changes, spread over a large population, really do make a major difference. And we can invite people into partnerships. Sharing the work and the dream always generates hope. It's why communities can accomplish more than individuals alone. It's why Martin Luther King's work helped change this country's attitudes and laws. It's the reason a small group of disciples two thousand years ago began to change the world. It's why thousands are turning out this weekend to hear the Dalai Lama speak about compassion. It is indeed why people join communities of faith.

Hope is the thing with feathers that perches in the soul and sings the tune without the words and never stops at all—as Emily Dickinson put it. Hope gives people the courage to change. We're here because we know, deep in our soul, that a different world is possible—a world where all human beings can live together with enough to eat, and dignified employment. We can accomplish all this in a way that celebrates the diversity in which we are created. We can build a world that's sustainable, that will not leave our children or theirs worse off than we are. We can heal this planet—with hope.

New Hope

Fresno, California, USA
San Joaquin Convention

29 March 2008

This was the reorganizing gathering for a group of Episcopalians whose bishop and other diocesan leaders had left the Church several months earlier, after nearly two decades of increasingly difficult relationships with the larger Church. The community was grieving as well as beginning to find some hope.

Acts 4:13–21; Psalm 118:19–24; Mark 16:9–15, 20

I bring you Easter greetings, good news of the resurrection of our Lord Jesus Christ. As he says repeatedly to his disciples, "Peace be with you," and "fear not." These may have been trying and traumatic months, but you are already clearly experiencing resurrection.

There is new hope here for a church that can tolerate and even welcome diversity. There is new hope for a reconciled community. There is above all new hope that this part of the body of Christ can focus on the needs of neighbors who need to hear the good news of God in Christ.

The varied band of people Jesus gathered around himself, those he healed, fed, and taught, was a surprisingly motley crew: tax collectors, political zealots—some who called for violent revolution—women, Jews and Samaritans, fishermen, shepherds, and more than a few Gentiles. They were as diverse as those of different groups in this part of God's vineyard. Jesus was the common reason for their community, as he is for ours. And if that body could come together, then there is hope for us.

Those disciples brought others with them, and they had their struggles, as we do, over who was acceptable and who was not. As Mark's account puts it, "'Teacher, we saw someone casting out demons in your name, and we tried to stop him, because he was not following us.' But Jesus said, 'Do not stop him; for no one who does a deed of power in my name will be able soon afterward to speak evil of me.

Whoever is not against us is for us'" (9:38–40). Whoever is doing God's work is not beyond the possibility of relationship. Be generous in your welcome and in your reconciling work.

Those early disciples struggled in other ways, too. Not long after the resurrection, the great controversy was about whether or not Gentiles could be part of this gathering. It led to the first great council in Jerusalem, which didn't easily or fully resolve the issue. The struggles have not stopped since—either in Jerusalem or in the wider church. Yet when we are bound in the fellowship of the body of Christ, miracles of fellowship and reconciliation are indeed possible.

The work ahead of this diocese in the coming months will be about identity, reconciliation, and mission. In other words, as you seek a renewed life together in Christ, you will be invited to remember who and whose you are, why you're here, and what you're going to do about it. A useful shorthand might be: identity, vocation, and mission as members of the body of Christ. I have just a few reminders as you seek answers to those questions:

- *Jesus is Lord.* In the same sense that Jesus, and not Caesar, is Lord, remember that no one else—not any hierarch, not any one of you—is Lord. We belong to God, whom we know in Jesus, and there is no other place we find the ground of our identity.

- *We are all made in the image of God.* Even when we can't see that image of God immediately, we are challenged to keep searching for it, especially in those who may call us enemy. There is pain and hurt here to be reconciled, and searching for the image of God in those we have offended and who have offended us is a central part of our reconciling vocation.

- *In baptism we discover that we are meant to be for others, in the same way that God is for us.* Jesus is the best evidence of that. And that means that God's mission must be our center of attention, not our own hurt or indeed anything that focuses on our own selves to the exclusion of our neighbor. For when we miss our neighbor, we miss God. I believe you are already discovering that God is healing old wounds as you work together. The work is just beginning, and it may not be easy, but it is essential. Focusing on the other, the ones outside this body, will be a vital part of discovering resurrection. Archbishop William Temple famously said that this church is the only human institution that exists primarily for the good of those outside of it. There is plenty of need here in this part of California—among migrant workers, single parents, young people with little sense of future or direction, returning veterans. Put your eyes on Jesus in the form of those strangers, and you will find resurrection.

- *And, finally, remember that you are not alone.* This part of the Body of Christ is only one limb. The rest of the Episcopal Church is with you, and will continue to be with you. A few people from other parts of this Church have joined you here today as incarnate evidence of the love of Christ, known in community. We stand with you in the firm and constant hope that this body will grow and flourish and bless the central valley of California in ways you have not yet dreamed of. And we will celebrate with you as that becomes reality.

Alleluia! Christ is risen.

Healing Planet Earth

Seattle, Washington, USA
Healing Our Planet Earth:
Stewardship of the Earth

12 April 2008

The opening lecture of the HOPE conference, to which people came from across the Church to think, learn, and strategize about how to help heal planet Earth.

Why have we called on the various parts of creation around here to teach us and show us the way? God's image is visible and detectible in all parts of creation; God is author of all. I was deeply struck by an image in Gary Lagerloef's retelling of Genesis:

Gravity reached out her tentative fingers.
Random pockets of denser stuff,
With time, fell into clumps and strands
Of billions of proto-galaxies.
The first stars formed,
And light shown again in the heavens,
Like birthday candles, arrayed
To celebrate a billion years of cosmic evolution.
And God said "It's looking better all the time!"[14]

"Gravity's tentative fingers . . ." and later, "with time, gravity cast her net again, gathering dust into new star systems." Gravity is not a bad image for God's lure, God's eternal desire for relationship—the weak force, and the nuclear force, and the attractive chaos that brings human beings together in relationship. Gravity is actually a very good translation of the Hebrew word for God's glory—*kabod*. It means heaviness, weightiness; it is something so substantial you can't help but notice. When we encounter the hand of God at work in the world about us, we are recognizing the glory of God. As the psalm we heard puts it, God "collects the waves of the ocean, and gathers up the depths of the sea."[15] We know God as the one who creates, we see the evidence of divine working in everything we encounter, and we know God in that lure for relationship, that engagement, enticement, fascination with all that is—God's tractor beam drawing us in.

The latter part of Psalm 104 (24–31) is one of the best scriptural summaries I know of that lure:

> O Lord, how manifold are your works!
> In wisdom you have made them all; the earth is full of your creatures.
> Yonder is the sea, great and wide, creeping things innumerable are there,
>   living things both small and great.
> There go the ships, and Leviathan that you formed to sport in it.
> These all look to you to give them their food in due season;
>   when you give to them, they gather it up;
>   when you open your hand, they are filled with good things.
> When you hide your face, they are dismayed;
>   when you take away their breath, they die and return to their dust.
> When you send forth your spirit, they are created;
>   and you renew the face of the ground.
> May the glory of the Lord endure forever; may the Lord rejoice in his works.

Let's look at that home of Leviathan as an image for the whole creation, because it's the creative womb from which life on this earth sprang. It's also the part of God's creation I know best. Yonder is the sea, great and wide, filled with living things small and great. And that sea just over yonder is increasingly subject to unholy consequences of our mindless fiddling and frolicking.

When I was in grade school, I remember being told that the oceans would solve the world's protein problem. In the same way that Norman Borlaug's green revolution began to increase cereal crop output in the Americas, Africa, and Asia, the sea would be our salvation. Indeed 15 percent of the world's protein does come from the sea, yet only 22 percent of the world's fisheries are managed in a sustainable way. If current fishing trends continue, essentially all of the world's fish stocks will collapse within fifty years. Since the beginning of commercial-scale fishing, the numbers of large predatory fish have been reduced to 10 percent of what they were before commercial-scale fishing began. This part of the world knows something about that in the history of salmon fishing. Reports from little more than a hundred years ago speak of fish so densely packed in coastal streams that they formed a virtual bridge from bank to bank. Thirty years ago I saw a stream like that on Kodiak Island. I doubt you can see it anywhere today. European immigrants in this part of the world harvested salmon with horse-drawn trawls, and very quickly nearly wiped them out in most river systems.

There are similar stories in many other parts of the world—the former cod fishery off the Grand Banks, the herring fishery in the North Sea, the anchovy fishery off Peru. More recently, historically abundant fisheries off Africa and in the South Pacific have been largely destroyed by commercial fishing methods. Bishop George Packard tells me of native Episcopalians in Micronesia who report that factory trawlers descend on their islands and virtually vacuum the seas. It's no longer possible to make a living by subsistence fishing there.

The difficulty is not just near shore. Commercial trawling is moving down the continental slopes, into waters up to a thousand meters deep, with devastating results. Not only are the long-lived and slow-growing fish and invertebrates quickly disappearing, but the habitat destruction from the trawls means that recovery will be unlikely even if fishing were to stop immediately.

Offshore fisheries are sweeping the seas clean, and a number of the fishery methods also denude the oceans of species that are not commercially targeted. Most Americans learned years ago about the problems of tuna seining that also caught spinner porpoises. Long-line fisheries, which use miles-long fences of baited hooks, catch birds, sharks, marine mammals, and tortoises, as well as fish both marketable and not. Indiscriminate use of those long lines is likely to lead to the extinction of a number of species.

But human impacts on the oceanic creation are not limited to fisheries. The largest scale problem is anthropogenic climate change, and those effects are significant to the oceans. Worldwide, right now, every square meter of the earth's surface gets an annual input of heat energy that exceeds the heat that's reflected back into space by about 0.8 watt. That's a very small light bulb over each square meter of surface, but there's no other place for the heat to go. The ocean can absorb a certain amount of heat, and so can the land, and eventually it will balance out, but not until the average temperature over the whole planet has increased significantly.

Heat input in the oceans has a couple of immediate effects—especially on the intensity of storms, particularly hurricanes and typhoons. The number and intensity of hurricanes off the Gulf and Atlantic coasts has risen by 75 percent since the 1970s. Katrina, Rita, and Wilma were the most recent examples. The first hurricane ever recorded in the South Atlantic occurred in 2004. The year 2005 had the most hurricanes ever recorded in the North Atlantic, as well as the most intense Atlantic storm, Hurricane Wilma.

Another major impact of global climate change on the oceans has to do with ice—and its melting. The Arctic is warming much faster than most other parts of the world ocean, in a positive feedback loop. Ice reflects most radiation back into space, and therefore keeps the water below it cooler. As the ice melts, the water absorbs ever more radiation. That warming also has an impact on cloud cover, which has been significantly reduced in recent years, leading to even higher thermal radiation input. The Northwest Passage is increasingly ice-free in summer; and is expected to be consistently available by about 2030. In August last summer it became fully navigable for the first time to ships without an icebreaker. Why is this important? In addition to contributing to increased rates of warming, it likely means the demise of polar bears, seals, and other animals that depend on the ice, which will further change polar ecosystems, their species composition and interactions. One consequence is reduced availability of traditional food sources for native peoples. Aside from the justice issues of eliminating those food sources, as those people migrate looking for sustenance and employment, they lose their cultures. About 90 percent of the indigenous languages in North America are very likely to disappear. That is a loss of God's creativity that is just as significant as the loss of endangered species.

There are other ice issues as well. The presence of significant amounts of ice on Greenland and Antarctica is the result of a shift in global climate patterns over geologic time. Under a different climate regime, that ice was a liquid part of the ocean. As it melts, it will contribute to a rise in ocean level. If all the ice on Greenland were to melt, sea level would rise about seven meters—about twice as much change as human beings have known in recorded history—and more than enough to inundate a number of South Pacific nations, New Orleans, New York, Amsterdam, Tokyo, Venice, most of coastal Bangladesh, and a lot of other port cities. Fortunately, the Antarctic doesn't seem to be melting quite as fast—yet—but melting of all the Antarctic ice sheets would raise sea level about seventy-five meters—well over our heads here. A sea level rise of only ten meters would flood about 25 percent of the U.S. population, primarily on the Gulf and East Coasts. In the last twenty-five years, global sea levels have risen around five centimeters, and twenty centimeters since 1900, along with about one degree Celsius rise in global temperature.[16]

There are a number of peculiar and significant issues in the ocean related to rising carbon dioxide levels, in addition to warming effects and a rise in sea level. The biggest one has to do with increasing acidity as carbon dioxide dissolves, because some of it turns into carbonic acid. The oceans are presently absorbing about two billion tons of CO_2 each year, a significant fraction of the annual emissions of seven billion tons. But there is a limit to how much carbon the oceans can absorb. At some point the oceans are likely to become more stratified, limiting absorptive capacity, and eventually they will even begin to give off carbon dioxide into the atmosphere as the oceans continue to warm. We're already seeing a significant change in pH, and beginning to see some impacts on marine organisms. As the pH decreases, it becomes metabolically more difficult to produce a calcareous (a particular form of calcium) skeleton. Some kinds of tiny phytoplankton, shelled animals like snails and clams, and corals will disappear, particularly in warmer waters. There are other animals who produce a different kind of carbonate skeleton, of a mineral called aragonite, who are likely to be threatened even sooner—pearl oysters and abalone are good examples.

The impacts on coral are multiple. Not only do rising sea temperatures lead to the local extinction of particular coral species, but they often cause "bleaching," which is the death of commensal algae living in a symbiotic relationship with the coral organism. Those algae contribute to the health of the coral, and the coral weaken if the algae die. The change in ocean acidity makes it more difficult for the corals to build skeletons, and increased storm strength leads to greater damage to coral reefs. I hope you begin to see the interrelated effects of climate change, just on one part of this global ecosystem. The effects extend to human communities as well—the ones that depend on reefs for food, coastal protection from storms, tourism economies, and effects much farther distant.

As the oceans warm and their pH changes, the fauna and flora may become locally extinct, or may move toward cooler waters (toward the poles or into greater depths). Warming oceans may become more vertically stable, reducing the amount of upwelling, which in good years brings nutrients to the surface and contributes to the ordinarily massive productivity off coasts like this one. The shift in species composition, whether due to climatic displacement or overfishing, often leads to a reduction in diversity. One of the truisms of the study of ecosystems, whether oceanic or terrestrial, is that the more diverse they are, the healthier and more stable they are likely to be. Reducing the biological diversity usually reduces the system's ability to adapt to change or unusual environmental pressure. Disruption often leads to the emergence of opportunistic species—like weeds in a newly plowed field. In overfished ecosystems, the slower-growing fish are often replaced by faster-growing species like jellyfish or squid, which may prevent the recovery of the fish stocks even when fishing pressure is reduced.

Disrupted ecosystems are also prone to boom-and-bust population cycles. Algal and phytoplankton blooms are examples, but other organisms also bloom—like those jellyfish who flourish when their fish predators are missing. This kind of excessive production can lead to rapid die-offs and oxygen exhaustion in the water as all that organic matter decays. When the low oxygen patch gets big, it's called a dead zone—and there are growing patches like this around the world, particularly around the North Atlantic. Significant dead zones exist in the Gulf of Mexico, related to overproduction, to silting after major storms, and to excess nutrients in river runoff. Others exist off the east coast, related to garbage and sewage dumping.

Chesapeake Bay is increasingly prone to this as well, and it has had major impacts on the crab and oyster fisheries there.

The loss of genetic diversity in an ecosystem has consequences for the other members of the system, as well as for species that may seem far removed. For one, human beings may lose access to unique characteristics of that ecosystem—drugs that may cure cancer, antitoxins, antibiotics, and the like. Creation has its own intrinsic worth, often beyond our imagining, and when it's gone, it's gone forever. As ecosystems are disrupted, undoubted myriads of species will be destroyed, many of which we have not yet even recognized, described, or named.

There are less obvious and ancillary consequences to our burgeoning presence and impact on oceanic ecosystems. Ship traffic is increasing exponentially. If you look at a map of the annual commercial shipping, it soon looks much like a nighttime picture of the earth—the lights or ship tracks are concentrated in very narrow bands. Ship strikes on whales are contributing significantly to increased mortality among a number of species, including the critically endangered northern right whale, already decimated nearly extinct from whaling in the early twentieth century.

That growing ship traffic also spreads invasive organisms around the world—things like zebra mussels, which contribute to marine fouling as they enter new environments. Shipping also spreads garbage, spills a variety of toxic fluids, and leaks pollutants like anti-fouling hull paint—all as a function of "normal" operations, not just because of oil spills, container losses, hull breakup, or sinking. Almost all commercial shipping today relies on fossil fuels for propulsion, which add to the carbon emission load.

We haven't even begun to explore the issues that rise from land-sea interactions, particularly as human beings alter near-shore environments. Construction, runoff, sewage, the use of ocean water for cooling, desalination, dredging, impacts on estuaries that reduce the diversity or health of their ecosystems—those are just a few of the ways in which human activity affects near-shore oceanic systems. Think for just a moment about the vast quantities of human produce that were washed back into the Gulf of Mexico after Katrina—houses, cars and boats, trees and land plants, garbage, bricks, television antennas, gasoline, livestock. In many parts of the Gulf Coast that outwash has effectively produced a toxic waste dump just offshore. We are beginning to recognize that the oceans are not the limitless receptacle or resource we long thought they were. The oceans are in fact beginning to groan.

If we can begin to hear that grave lament, we may recover some ability to partner in renewing the playground of Leviathan. The hope we have in us contains the seeds of a renewed creation. The sea water that runs in our veins—and our tissue has virtually the same elemental composition as the oceans—may remind us that we are created of the dust of the earth, dissolved in the moist breath of God. We are intimately connected to all parts of what Sallie McFague calls the body of God. Creation is groaning in travail. But it is not the travail of childbirth. It's the groaning of mortal illness. We must hear that cry, and respond.

There is much we can do, in small and large ways. We can pay attention to what we eat. Learn what fisheries are sustainable and which are not, and alter your buying habits appropriately. Eating lower on the food chain helps as well. Advocate for appropriate management systems—adequate marine reserves, closed to all fishing, that can provide a sanctuary and help to repopulate overfished and damaged areas. Limit fishery methods; use permits, licenses, and quotas to reduce the fishing pressure. Recover a sense that we are all responsible for the whole, and don't let our neighbors devolve into the tragedy of the commons. When no one owns or acts as steward of a resource, there is little economic incentive for anyone to act responsibly. People of faith have a moral incentive that grows out of our understanding that we are all part of one much greater whole.

We must also learn more environmentally responsible ways of growing fish and shellfish commercially. Salmon farms may produce cheap and relatively consistent supplies for a while, but in some parts of the world they are almost wholly unregu-lated. In Chile, for example, culture methods have led to recent outbreaks of para-sites and microbial infections that are not only killing most of the farmed salmon, but threatening wild stocks and polluting the environment. The usual commercial response has been to simply move to another location and start the cycle over again. Learn where your seafood comes from, and demand a higher standard of environmentally accountable production. In the same way that shade-grown and fairly traded coffee has improved the lives of others, accountable aquaculture can change the lives of Chilenos and many people in Asia.

The connections between economics and ecology are vast, complex, and foundational to a society built on justice. One not so small example points to the interconnections between Tijuana, Mexico and San Diego, California. The two border cities have equivalent populations, but the per capita municipal budget is sixteen times higher north of the border. San Diego has state-of-the-art sewage treatment, but south of the border overflows frequently pollute the Tijuana River and the Pacific Ocean on the U.S. side of the border. A wall will not solve that border crossing problem, either.

Indeed, water use and the availability of clean water is likely to be the most sig-nificant environmental and economic justice issue in the coming decades—in the forms of fresh water, effluent, and the marine environment. The Colorado River is one example—so much of its flow is used on the U.S. side that the outflow into

the Sea of Cortez is often dry—and the ecology of that long embayment is changing. Use of the Columbia River's water is another issue, with justice implications
for native peoples, fisheries, and farmers, as well as environmental implications for
human beings who live all along its reaches and the marine species who live outside
its mouth. Those interconnections, and the passion in this part of the world for
working on them, are why the Episcopal Church intends to put an environmental
and economic justice officer here.

I've pointed to a number of ways in which human activity is having negative
impacts on the marine environment. Some of it is clearly the result of greed, and
a fair bit of it is unintended or unrecognized consequence—the human desire for
food, transport, and a clean place to live: send the garbage elsewhere, not in my
backyard. Those consequences will continue, and their impact will increase, as
long as we see the oceans as dumping grounds and places to be exploited. That's
not why God put us on this planet.

The historic Western misinterpretation of that directive in Genesis—be fruitful, multiply, and subdue the earth—along with the way some of the Protestant
reformers claimed creation as their promised reserve, are responsible for a great
deal of that exploitative behavior. People of faith, particularly the heirs of those
misinterpretations, have a critical responsibility to recover, or rediscover, the
underlying Hebraic and tribal traditions that point to the value of community
over independent and disconnected individuals. All the Pauline language about
the body of Christ applies equally to the body of God's creation. We are all part
of one larger body. None of us lives for him or herself alone, and indeed our very
meaning is dependent on our relationships with God and other. Our Trinitarian
theology says that social relationships are innate to God's very identity.

That passage in Genesis about filling the earth and subduing it closes like this:
" . . . have dominion over the fish of the sea and over the birds of the air and over
every living thing that moves upon the earth" (Gen 1:28). Having dominion does
mean to rule, but in the way God rules, not in the way of earthly rulers. "Dominion" is related to *domus*—a house, a temple, even the dome over the earth. We all
live under that same dome, and caring for one's fellow inhabitants is the sign of
a wise and holy householder. That kind of steward operates out of compassion,
living beyond self, caring for the children to the seventh generation. That kind of
ruler cares for the people of this generation and of the next, and does not ignore
the pain and suffering of fellow creatures. We are a people of incarnation, and
abundant life is meant for this world and this life—for all creation.

Why are we here? To give glory to God.

How do we do that? By acknowledging the gravity of the current situation, and
the pull of God's gravity back into right relationship.

What gets in the way? Fear, timidity, greed, selfishness, laziness and ignorance. Mostly, though, what gets in the way is a lack of compassion for our fellow creatures, as we treat them in a way that ignores their gravity, their substantial and unique reflection of God's own creative glory.

What next? In a minute you'll hear a very brief reading from Hildegard of Bingen, who talks about greenness. The word in this translation is "verdancy," though it's often left in its original Latin form, *viriditas*. As she expands on that meaning, it is the explicit expression of God's creative glory. *Viriditas* is the creative force in all that is. It is that which leads to resurrection, to new life born out of death, to the rising life of Jesus, to the ever-present Spirit urging us, luring us, drawing us into creative relationship with God and all God's creation. You and I are meant to be partners in God's glorious creative work. How will you be green, and heal this planet, and give glory to God?

God in Community

Louisville, Kentucky, USA
Diocese of Kentucky
17–18 May 2008

A diocesan visit to a fascinating part of the world, far greener than the desert I talk about here, but with its own desert character in the leanness of many lives, particularly in Appalachia. I was there on the feast of the Trinity, which is most specifically about God as relationship.

Feast of the Trinity: Genesis1:1–2: 3; 2
Corinthians 13:5–14; Matthew 28:16–20

I was in Phoenix earlier this week for a meeting about poverty in the United States. Thursday morning I went out for a run, up a mountain that looms north of the retreat center. Early in the morning before the sun comes up in the desert, there are lots of birds greeting the day, and as it gets light, you can begin to see the myriad kinds of strange plants. The desert in that part of the southwest is filled with the strange products of creation—maybe God's sense of humor at play.

There's a plant called ocotillo, a tall, whip-like cactus, which looks like a bunch of sticks growing like a vase out of the same spot in the ground. Much of the year it looks dead, but when there's been a little rain, leaves may begin to grow on it—little green leaves that last a few weeks and then dry up and fall off. Every once in a while, the plant blooms, with great big red, bird-shaped blossoms along those empty and leafless stalks. There were a few of those, past their blooming prime and without any leaves. Those dead-looking sticks can become a glorious reminder of the creative and playful reality of God. Yet that plant also bears sharp and abundant spines, and it would make a fitting crown of thorns.

That desert is also home to lots and lots of saguaros. If you remember those old westerns, or the comic strip Snoopy, you'll remember those big tall cactuses that loom twenty feet and more into the air. Snoopy's brother Spike is usually sitting under one of them when he's reading a letter. Right now many of them are blooming in the Sonoran desert—great big white blossoms at the ends of those branches way up in the air. Those blooms open in the middle of the night and last only a day or two; they're reported to smell pretty good, but you'd need a ladder truck to get close enough to tell. Those saguaros are not a bad image of Trinity, for they become little communities or ecosystems in themselves. That long-lived plant grows very slowly, and it dominates the landscape. As it ages, other creatures bore holes in its trunk and limbs, and set up housekeeping—things like burrowing owls and insects and lizards and woodpeckers. They help fertilize the plant on which they live. Those flowers attract bats and insects, to pollinate, produce seeds, and continue the cycle. The plant itself is source of life for others who dwell in its branches; it attracts other creatures into an interdependent life.

The image of God as Trinity is really about relationship and community. That's what Rublev's great icon shows—three divine beings sitting in a circle, heads inclined toward one another, yet also seeming to invite the viewer into the circle. When we talk about a creator who becomes human in Jesus, and continues to send Spirit, we are talking about God with us, a God who in God's own being models a relational community.

That is why we baptize in the name of the Trinity. That language about Father, Son, and Holy Spirit is not merely about getting the words right. It is about recognizing, deep down, that when we welcome another into this community called the Body of Christ, we acknowledge that we depend on one another and we will be changed by the presence of this new member.

Even in that gospel mandate to go and baptize, we see the importance of a diverse and relational community. The eleven disciples go to the mountain where Jesus told them to go, and "they worshiped him, but some doubted." Why didn't the early Christians focus on their unanimity? Well, probably because no human community has ever been completely of one mind and voice. But more than that, the doubt and worship are part of the same response to God. If all we did in response to something we perceived as God was to worship, we would certainly end up practicing idolatry—at least some of the time. The doubters play a vital role in keeping communities honest. Woe betide a community without doubters—it will almost certainly become a mob, hell-bent on imposing its will on others.

The Anglican family is seeing something like that right now in Zimbabwe, where the president, Robert Mugabe, seems to have lost the primary election, and is facing a runoff. He and his followers are apparently trying to stifle and silence the opposition, or indeed any part of society that's not under their direct control. The Anglican Church of Zimbabwe has been caught up in the mess for several years. The last bishop of Harare, a close associate and strong supporter of Mugabe, was deposed a year or so ago, and continues to occupy many church buildings, even though the courts there have ordered his followers to share the space. Clergy and parishioners who no longer look to him as bishop are being beaten, arrested, and harassed. Last Sunday the police came and beat up parishioners in one of those churches while they were standing in line to receive communion. The Mothers' Union responded by starting to sing—a clear reminder that as frightened as they were individually, together they can remember that God is there in the midst of their suffering. Pray for the people of Harare, for they are part of us.

Trinity says God is relationship. Zimbabweans are part of us, and we are part of them—so much so that it challenges our Western focus on the supremacy of the individual. We live in a society that still insists that my rights are the most important thing, that I can do whatever I want unless it causes immediate harm or injury to another, and that my individual decisions have little impact on others. Trinity reminds us of a truth known to the ancient tribes of Israel—that we are more as members of community than we are as individuals, and that our individual salvation depends on the salvation of the whole. There's a Zulu word for it—*ubuntu*. You may have heard Archbishop Desmond Tutu use it. We might translate it as, "I am because we are." It is fundamental to our understanding of the Body of Christ: When one part of the body suffers, all do; when one rejoices, we all rejoice.

This diocese knows something about ubuntu, and life in the Trinity. Your work in Jubilee ministries, your focus on MDGs, say that if we would be a healed people, we have to do something about the suffering of others. You know yourselves as Korean and Sudanese and African-American and Karen (a Burmese tribe) as well as Anglo. You know yourselves connected with people in the diocese of Byumba, Rwanda, and with the Church of Scotland. You continue to search for the image of God in people who may seem at first to be unlike you. When Augustine said, "Our hearts are restless until they find their rest in thee, O Lord," he was pointing toward that relational and trinitarian understanding of God. If we, individually or as a community, want to participate in God, then we must be restless until all have found rest, comfort, and healing in that holy community of God.

That's what Paul is telling the folks in Corinth as he says good bye. This translation says: "Put things in order, listen to my appeal, agree with one another, live in peace; and the God of love and peace will be with you." We might just as well translate it as "Mend the world. While you're at it, cheer up, because with a common mind, you *will* find peace and know that God is with you." Above all, it's a reminder that together they can and will know the presence of God in their midst. Mend the world, and find the peace that passes understanding.

Baptized into the Trinity (the community of God), and doing what Jesus taught us (love one another as I have loved you), and remembering that God is with us, we will know healing and wholeness and holiness. Even in the midst of life that is as threatening and foreign as the spines of a giant cactus, we know that God is at work calling us into relationship.

Wise as Serpents, Innocent as Doves

Cuddesdon, England
Transforming Episcope
closing Eucharist, Ripon College

11 July 2008

At this conference on the ministry of women as bishops, the task was to hearten, encourage, those who will still wait years before they see one of their sisters clothed as a bishop.

Hosea 14:2–9; Psalm 80:1–7; Matthew 10:16–23

Stir up your might, O Lord, and come to save us. Restore us, let your face shine, that we may be saved. (Ps 80 2–3)

I imagine that prayer has been said many times by those in this room. And perhaps even more often the prayer, "How long, O Lord, how long?"

Well, stir up your courage, my sisters—and my brothers. God is at work, even when you can't see the seed growing or hear the angel speaking in the night. The faithfulness you need in order to endure comes from God. This struggle is not new, yet you are soon to be delivered—soon enough, in God's time. Those who endure to the end will be saved.

There is plenty of fear here and around the Anglican Communion just now—don't let it be yours. Jesus may say, "Don't worry about how you're going to speak or what you're going to say," but the BBC wanted my sermon texts for Sunday ten days in advance! My reply was, "The Spirit isn't working quite that far ahead of time." To which, of course, they answered, "Well, we are responsible for every word that goes out over these broadcasts . . . " Fear seems to be equal opportunity, free-floating, not just here, but almost anywhere there are human beings struggling with truth and their take on ultimate meaning.

"I'm sending you out like sheep into the midst of wolves, so be wise as serpents and innocent as doves," says Jesus. Are we sheep among the wolves? And if so, does that mean rolling over and playing dead? Well, what gifts do sheep have?

Wool—lots of it at the right time of the year—that might just stick in a wolf's throat if it's long enough. And if a whole bunch of sheep get together, they can defend themselves against a wolf, even pretty aggressively. But I don't think Jesus is encouraging striking the wolf with hooves or butting it to death. Instead, it's that ability to get together that is the greatest gift the sheep have—that herding instinct that can put the weakest in the center and gather the strong all around for protection. Don't put anybody out there all alone.

Sheep can survive on pretty meager grazing—goats are even better at it, but most of the biblical writers have a pretty dim view of goats—they're seen as too smart for their own good, most of the time. But sheep can find food, and even thrive, in places that look a lot like a desert. How will this flock keep finding adequate grazing, and support one another in the process? Who are the shepherds who will keep the flock moving between oases? Sheep—care for your shepherds. Shepherds—tend your flocks.

And what about the wolves? I'm not so sure they're our opponents. I think the wolves have a lot more to do with what we fear most—and most of that is internal. The wolves don't get the upper hand unless the sheep have stopped paying attention to the shepherd and scattered. Wolves have to find prey to survive; sheep don't have to cooperate. That take on things sometimes looks like what the Canon to the Ordinary in Nevada used to call "malicious compliance" or "subversive over-compliance." It underlies all of Jesus' language about walking the extra mile and giving away your coat and turning the other cheek, so the person who slaps it must recognize you equally as a human being.

Be wise as serpents—lie there in the sun, looking lazy, taking in everything that's going on. Listen to the vibrations of marchers far away, notice the odors of fear, sense the heat of those advancing, and take to your holes when you have to. And be innocent as doves—like Jesus, go around unprotected by the violent response to fear. Fly above it.

What if all the women clergy of the Church of England took a Sunday off? What would happen if they and all their supporters stayed away? Do you think the Church would notice? A CNN reporter noticed something quite interesting this week. He said, "Well, thirteen hundred clergy may have said they're leaving the Church of England if it consents to women bishops, but I couldn't find anybody at the Synod who would say why. There was no representative of that position anywhere to be found." Sometimes the doves get above the fray, and ask the awkward questions.

Maybe you know the story of the women of the Niger Delta. Oil exploitation in that part of the world has devastated villages, poisoned the drinking water and the fish by spilling crude oil. The flares that burn off excess gas pollute the atmosphere and cover everything with soot. The villagers worked for years to get the oil companies to change their habits. They were in a bind, for they had nowhere else to go, and they had long depended on the fruits of the earth and sea to survive. They pleaded and picketed, and some even tried destroying the pipes and machinery. Nothing worked. Finally a large group of women marched down to the corporate offices, sat down outside the building, and took off their shirts. They didn't shame themselves; in that culture they shamed anyone who saw them, and they shamed their opposition into action. The oil companies began to negotiate.

Doves can fly above the gathering armies, and spend their energy where it will do the most good. They can't do much to defend themselves on the ground; their safety lies in a larger perspective. Wise as serpents, innocent as doves. We've just watched Ingrid Betancourt and several other hostages delivered from years of captivity in the jungles of Colombia. If what we saw was accurate, it was a pretty wily operation that somehow managed to avoid violence—only by the grace of God. I'm not convinced the hostages would not have resorted to violence if something had gone wrong, but their escape is the kind of crafty wisdom for which snakes are known.

Ingrid and her fellow captives endured years in the jungle, feeling pretty despondent. Who else tells a story like that—lost, misunderstood, abandoned? Hagar's story is similar—but remember that she and her offspring also received a blessing and promise from God. The woman who met Jesus at the well is a witness to that kind of endurance, and so were Hildegard and the other women mystics of the Middle Ages.

You walk in the footsteps of the wise women burned at the stake for being uppity enough to think they could heal people. Your witness and solidarity mean that you hold the hands of the trafficked and the abandoned ones. Your preaching can speak the pain and injustice of women and girls mutilated or married too young "for cultural reasons," and women of all ages raped by the doers of war. And you are also the sister of the forty-one-year-old mother who just made the Olympic swimming team in four events—Dara Torres may seem as strong as the teenagers, though not for long—but she *is* far wiser.

You are building that vision Hosea speaks, of Israel blossoming like the lily, lush as the forests of Lebanon. You are building a community fruitful and fragrant, flourishing with abundance for a feast. Keep nourishing that vision, not with the warrior's tools, but with the wiliest and most challenging creations of the spirit you can muster. Those who endure will ultimately be blessed.

Caught in the Net

Staten Island, New York, USA
St. Andrew's Episcopal Church
Feast of Andrew

30 November 2008

A warm and friendly welcome to a three-hundred-year-old congregation, even on a dark and stormy night with a procession through the rain. For me, an opportunity to round the circle, as I came into the Episcopal Church and was confirmed at St. Andrew's, Murray Hill, New Jersey, and, like Andrew, am still fishing.

Deuteronomy 30:11–14; Psalm 34; Romans 10:8b–18; Matthew 4:18–22

It's an honor and a privilege to be with you for this celebration of three hundred years of faithful witness on this island. As I travel around this Church I am continually amazed and delighted to discover the ways in which we are all connected. Last night I found some more of those connections. Your warmth and welcome tied us together in new ways. We are all truly part of one and the same Body of Christ.

I'd like to explore some of those connections, starting with Andrew. I was confirmed at St. Andrew's, across Arthur Kill in the Diocese of New Jersey. Quite a few years later, I was ordained priest on the feast of Andrew. The bishop of Oregon, Robert Ladehoff, who ordained me (three times), was himself consecrated on this feast two hundred years after Samuel Seabury. He's also the eight hundredth bishop after Seabury, the first bishop on this continent, who served here during and after the Revolutionary War. Seabury probably would have called it the colonial rebellion.

This congregation traces its origins to missionaries sent here from England just after 1700—prompted by the governor of New York and the rector of Trinity Wall Street. The Rev. Aeneas Mackenzie came and settled on Staten Island in 1704. He wrote back to London, urging the mission agency to send money for teachers, because there were no schools. The three teachers who were eventually hired taught white children in the daytime and slave children at night. Yes, there were large numbers of slaves here, and when a large estate was given to this parish in 1718, nearly half its value was counted in slaves. New York did not legally free all the slaves until 1827.

Aeneas Mackenzie and leading citizens laid plans for building a church and buying farm- and timberland to support the work. Queen Anne lent her support as well, sending a silver communion set and confirming the land transfers. The first church building was finished in 1711. The congregation included English-speaking colonists, but also French Huguenots and some Dutch speakers, apparently convinced to join by the minister's care for them and the fact that he had managed to acquire copies of the Book of Common Prayer translated into Dutch. Mr. Mackenzie was fishing mightily on this island, and even in New Jersey—some of his congregants came from Elizabethtown when the weather was good enough. He did his fishing not just in his own language or racial or economic group, but among all the people of this extended community. That kind of fishing still marks this congregation.

When Andrew first encounters Jesus, he is told to leave his fishnet and go fish for people. He may have walked off and left his net and boat, but he didn't lose the ability to draw in what he was looking for. Fishing for people has a lot to do with luring and making connections—not in a manipulative sense, but in offering the bait of loving kindness or reaching out a hand to someone in need. The kind of fishing that Aeneas Mackenzie did here answered the needs and desires of his fellow inhabitants—for education, for solace in the face of disease and death, for companionship and solidarity, and for hope in a hard land. The good news he shared brought comfort—strength is how it would have been understood then—and assurance that God cares for every single one. From all I read and hear, you are still doing that kind of fishing here today—sheltering the homeless, sharing solace with those who have lost companions, both human and animal, and sharing the hospitality of this house with all sorts and conditions of people. That kind of fishing knits us into the great net of Christ, building connections with each other in the love of God.

Samuel Seabury had a challenge on his hands when he first came here at the beginning of the Revolution. He was known to the residents as a crown loyalist, and he couldn't actually move here and hope to sleep peacefully in his bed. He kept living in Manhattan and plying his trade as a physician, but coming out here to preach and preside at services. At one point he ran off to Long Island to seek shelter with the British troops, and in response the colonists turned this place into a hospital and burned the pews. The community that follows Jesus never has been a shelter from conflict, a reality which Andrew also knew. I imagine you've had your share of conflict as well!

But this congregation persisted. St. Andrew's was the only church on the island that continued to hold services all through the war. Seabury ministered both to British soldiers and to American revolutionaries, and to those caught in the middle, and he continued to fish here after the Revolution was accomplished. As things began to settle down, his fellow Anglicans elected him to go to England and seek consecration as a bishop. The difference of opinion settled on these shores between revolutionaries and the British marked the beginning of a new nation, but it also represents the start of the Anglican Communion. Seabury was refused ordination in England and went to Scotland instead—where Andrew is patron saint. We continue as Episcopalians here because the Scots took pity on us, for they already knew something of what it means to be an occupied country.

I was in London for several days this past week, for a meeting of the Joint Standing Committee, a group that's related to the primates' meeting and the Anglican Consultative Council. We were there to talk about Anglican Communion issues, and we met at the Anglican Communion offices, in St. Andrew's House. Every year, on or near the feast of Andrew, the office there holds a celebration for friends and supporters. Tuesday night we celebrated the feast of Andrew with a Eucharist and dinner. I was asked to say grace before dinner, and I gave thanks for our gathering, and the food, and for Andrew. As dinner began, a Ugandan woman who is on the JSC came up to me and thanked me for praying for Andrew. She went on to say that her son who died last year was named Andrew. The prayer let her give thanks, even in the midst of her continuing grief. The warp and weft of this fish net in which we are all caught binds us together in ways beyond our imagining.

You and I are caught in a net that includes Episcopalians all over the United States, spiritual descendants of those early Church of England clergy and missionaries who first came to these shores four hundred years ago. We are caught in a net that includes Episcopalians in places like Taiwan and Micronesia, where others have spread the gospel much more recently. We are caught up with Episcopalians in Honduras, Ecuador, Venezuela, Colombia, Puerto Rico, Dominican Republic, Haiti, and the Virgin Islands, whose communities are a bit younger than yours, but just as faithful. And we are caught up with Episcopalians in six countries in Europe, whose congregations are mostly less than a hundred years old. But we are also caught up with Anglicans in Brazil, Mexico, Central America, the Philippines, and Liberia, whose churches trace their roots or branches to missionaries from the Episcopal Church. The Church in the Philippines began when the Brotherhood of St. Andrew sent missionaries there in 1892, and that saint still names their seminary.

We are linked with Anglicans in all parts of Africa, Asia, and Europe through their connections with England. The net that Andrew first began to knit, and Aeneas Mackenzie added to in this place, reaches around the world, and it's still catching people, here and far, far away. All of us are linked by those slender strands in the Body of Christ. When one strand in that net is stretched or broken, the rest of us feel it if we're paying attention. We notice—and grieve—when Christians in India are persecuted or killed for their faith, as we rejoice when peace comes in Ireland or South Africa.

Keep fishing, keep throwing out the net, keep reaching for the line called Jesus that knits us all into God's net. And give thanks for Andrew, first of the fishers of men—and women.

The Wonders of the Deep

New York, New York, USA
World Maritime Day, St. James Episcopal Church
25 October 2007

The International Maritime Organization is an advocacy group for mariners and the marine industries—shipping, fishing, and many others. We gave thanks for those ministries in the midst of a day devoted to the IMO's response to current environmental challenges.

Genesis 1:27–28, 31; Psalm 107:23–30; Matthew 4:18–22

I was in Puerto Rico last week to visit the Episcopal Church there, and I flew back early Sunday evening. As our plane left the island, I watched the sunset for thirty minutes through the towering clouds, as the sun painted everything—sky, clouds, and sea—in stunning and changing color. That unearthly display was the result of clear air and increasing altitude—we never get to see skies quite so blue or clouds so deeply salmon colored at sea level. It was on a different kind of vessel, in another ocean, and the opposite end of the day, but it was a powerful reminder of a sunrise I watched thirty years ago on a research vessel at sea north of Hawaii. There were flying fish on the deck, the same kind of towering pillars of clouds, but the colors were pastel rather than passionate. The poem I wrote was no match for Kipling's words, but it grew out of the same sense of awe that pushed him to talk about the dawn that "comes up like thunder outer China 'crost the Bay . . ." in *Mandalay*.[17]

It is the same kind of wonder the psalmist talks about—the works of the Lord and his wonders in the deep. That sense of wonder draws many of us to the sea, and it's the same pull that drew another poet, John Masefield, as he wrote, "I must go down to the seas again, to the lonely sea and the sky."[18] That wonder lies behind the attraction that continues to send some "down to the sea in ships, to ply their trade in deep waters."

The wonders of God's good creation, and the need we still have to make our living by the sweat of our brow, bring us here today to give thanks for the ministry of mariners, to pray for their safety, and to encourage all of us to care even more deeply for this wondrous planet on which we dwell.

That sense of awe at creation is an invitation into relationship with the creator. I think there's a reason Jesus started his ministry with fisherfolk, with guys who knew what it was like to suffer sun and wind and storm at sea, to revel in the lambent light of dawn, and to put up with a way of life that one day puts overwhelming abundance in the net and the next day nothing. Those who go to sea know that life is unpredictable, that the world is far larger than anything a human being can control, and that somehow all of it is shot through with unutterable beauty and grace.

Awe is a basic religious response, and if it's not squelched it can produce a deep desire for relationship—it sends us looking for more. Right after Jesus calls Peter, Andrew, James, and John, he launches out into Galilee, teaching, telling people the good news of God's presence, and healing them in body and mind. Presumably he's teaching those four fishermen at the same time: here, God has created this wondrous earth and all its inhabitants, and if you're going to follow me, then your job is to teach and heal, and help put everything back into right relationship.

Jews and Christians haven't spent a lot of time and energy talking about it in recent centuries, but a significant part of that work of putting things back into right relationship has to do with this planet and all its inhabitants, human and not. There are some wonderful images in the Hebrew prophets that talk about what a healed earth looks like—water springing up in the desert, lion and lamb living together without one of them seeing the other as dinner, or the sea roaring out its praise of the Lord.

The International Maritime Organization's focus this year is on healing the transportation base on which the whole maritime industry depends—or, rather, floats. That watery support has been polluted with oil and sewage, plastic and old ships, while the air above it is increasingly filled with gases that contribute to warming the whole planet. The living communities that depend on the ocean are suffering not just from pollution, but from overfishing, shifting chemistry, calefaction (profound localized warming) and changing weather patterns that are at least partly the result of planetary warming. Others who depend on the oceans, like native subsistence fishing communities, are going hungry because factory trawlers have exhausted their food source. Some human communities will likely lose their traditional homelands as sea level rises in the coming decades. There are island nations in the South Pacific whose average height above sea level is only six feet—and the dry land on which they dwell is beginning to shrink.

Jesus called those disciples, as he continues to call us, to tell people not only that God is among us and seeking relationship with us, but that we have something to do in response—to heal, cure, restore, make whole. Salvation, in its fullest sense, means just that—the wholeness, healing, and holiness of human beings in their fullness, but also the healing and restoration of all of creation. Over and over again we are reminded that as long as some are suffering, none of us can really be whole. Our salvation only comes with the salvation of all.

You and I have the ability to begin to heal this earth. When the first human beings were charged with dominion over the fish of the sea and the birds of the air and every living thing that moves on the earth, God did not intend for us to abuse those gifts, but to use and care well for them, so that they might continue to be a blessing for all God's creation. Our own lives, and those of our descendants, depend on how we care for the whole. Will we bless God in our stewardship of this earth, and bless all its inhabitants in the process? Or will we ignore our neighbors and foul this watery garden?

Peter and Andrew, James and John, and all the fishing fools who followed them, went down to the sea in ships, and plied their trade there, out of reverence for what God has created. Those disciples went fishing for people for the same reason—out of the reverent sense that God has blessed us and asks us to heal what is ill and broken. Healing the human race and all of creation means enough to eat—food that often comes in ships or from the sea itself; it means medical care and pharmaceuticals, drugs that may come from the riches of the sea; it means clean air to breathe and dignified employment and enough education to let us fall in love with learning about the wonders of this world. Above all, healing the world means the kind of peaceful community that can emerge only when all are fed, and whole, and living in right relationship with their neighbor. Right use of the riches of creation can bring peace and healing to the whole earth. It is blessed and entirely possible work. May we dream that dream of a sea that can roar out its blessing! May we dream of a world where all know God's peace and wholeness.

> Deep peace of the running wave to you.
> Deep peace of the flowing air to you.
> Deep peace of the quiet earth to you.
> Deep peace of the shining stars to you.
> Deep peace of the Son of Peace to you.[19]

> In the full tide of the day and in its ebbing,
> In the rising of the sun and its setting,
> The mighty God be with you
> The loving God protect you
> The holy God guide you
> And the blessing . . . [20]

Field of Dreams

London, England
St. Martin in the Fields
27 July 2008

I had an invitation to preach in this central London congregation in the middle of the Lambeth Conference. This congregation has a deep commitment to ministry with all the inhabitants of the city. They've just finished a building project that burrowed into the earth to provide more space in an environmentally friendly way. Their basement coffee shop is paved with the gravestones of those who have been buried there over several centuries.

1 Kings 3:5–12; Psalm 119:129–136; Romans 8: 26–34;
Matthew 13:31–33, 44–49a

It has been a joy to be in this country for the last two-and-a-half weeks. Two weeks ago I was in Salisbury, where we celebrated the 750th anniversary of their *new* cathedral. Part of that celebration involved a pilgrimage—a couple of miles' walk from the ruins of the old cathedral, excavated only in the last few decades, down into the town that has grown up around the new one. While I was there, the dean drove us past Stonehenge, where archaeologists continue to discover intriguing things about what life in this land was like three and four millennia ago.

The burials that have been excavated are informative both because of what scientists can learn from the bones, and because of what is buried with the dead— implements of daily life, jewels, weapons, a variety of items hidden in the grave to protect and guide the dead on their next journey. The treasures hidden in graves like those are valuable for what they teach us about the living, not for what they put in our bank accounts.

I have found all sorts of fascinating things in other fields in the western United States. I've found old crockery in a field around a house we lived in, left by settlers in the late 1800s. I've found Native American arrowheads exposed in other fields in that part of the world. In the last ten days in Canterbury, I've run past the Church of Saints Cosmus and Damian in the Blean and wondered about what is hidden in the moat and fields round that ancient church. The days we bishops spent in Canterbury Cathedral gave abundant evidence of the treasured bones buried in the earth and above it in that sacred place. Thomas Becket's shrine is a treasure of yet another sort.

What has St. Martin's found by digging in this field? Your excavation says something about the treasure discovered among the poor and the homeless, and the blessing that Jesus pronounced on the poor. The kingdom of heaven is indeed like the treasure hidden in this field, a treasure that you have gone and sold all you had—or convinced many donors to part with—in order to buy.

Jesus' parables this morning are so familiar that we've lost the sense of surprise and shock that his first hearers would have had. The kingdom of heaven is like a small seed that grows large and shelters the birds—the early Christians would have heard that and thought about Gentiles. This place and its work also shelter the unlikely and unnoticed and sometimes despised outsider.

The kingdom of heaven is like yeast that leavens everything around it. That would have been intensely shocking to Jesus' hearers, for it compares God's presence to something unclean that contaminates everything it touches. What metaphor would Jesus use here? Maybe he would say that the kingdom of heaven is like the odor of unwashed bodies, finding shelter at last in a well-heated room.

The kingdom of heaven is like finding something unexpected in a field, and selling all you've got in order to buy it. The kingdom of heaven is like searching the earth for a great treasure, and then giving all you have to own it. We can find that valuable thing accidentally or by diligent searching, but it will take all we have to possess it. It might be like letting your mission drive the use of these buildings, and the sacrificial giving that makes such remarkable work possible.

And finally, the kingdom of heaven is like a net full of fish. At the end of time, those fish will be sorted into useful ones and trash fish—but not until then. We don't know which is which, and until the end of things we might cultivate a perception that sees pearls of great price in all the oysters around us.

The kingdom of heaven is all around us, among us, in unsuspected places, in places where we might expect to find it if we look hard enough, and growing in ways we may find distasteful or surprising. A couple of nights ago, a group of young people moved into the next dormitory on the campus of the University of Kent. They were partying quite energetically when I went to bed. The noise woke me up at a quarter to three, and the loud screams and laughter continued until 5 a.m. I think Jesus would say the kingdom of heaven is like that, for their mirth and delight said a great deal about joy and peace, even if I had a hard time joining in.

In the last days, I've seen evidence of the kingdom of heaven among bishops who agree and disagree about the hot-button issues, among bishops who speak different languages, and among bishops who come from vastly different contexts. One bishop in Madagascar has told of a diocese that is devastated every year by cyclones, sometimes several times—yet he continues to work and rebuild. He holds a vision of a cathedral and churches that will be shelters from the storm, both literally and figuratively, and used for schools during the week. He says, "I will build more churches and fill them with the poor."

Another bishop in Sudan tells us about his people who are returning refugees, who have nothing—they cannot grow crops or feed themselves, and they are struggling to reestablish their lives. He also tells us of the presence of Al Qaeda, and large guns being carried south by nomads, and he recounts his fears that warfare will soon break out in even larger ways. Yet that bishop, and his brother bishops, continue to speak good news to their people, to tell their stories to others, and to seek our prayers and support, particularly from the nations of the world who may yet convince Sudan to care for all its people.

The kingdom of heaven is like 650 bishops marching through the streets of this city a couple of days ago, insisting that together we can end global poverty if we have the will to do it. Your prime minister shares that hope, and has pledged his assistance in very concrete ways, as he told us in a powerful speech on Thursday. The hope of ending poverty is like a mustard seed that can grow into a tree of life large and generous enough to shelter all the people of this world—but it will take lots of us to water and fertilize it.

Where and how do you look for the kingdom of heaven? It will take what is old and what is new—the good stuff from the past and the surprising possibilities of the present. This congregation already knows a great deal about where and how to look—the first radio broadcast of a religious service, the first lending library, building down into the earth in order to liberate and build up the people of this city. Even the reality that people of different faiths come together here regularly to pray and seek divine inspiration.

Where will you look in your own life? What treasure do you seek? What old thing must be preserved, and what new insight will be a clue to the kingdom of heaven around us? The struggle to answer those questions goes on throughout our own lives, in the church, and all around us. And the fish don't have to be sorted until the end of time. So fear not, keep looking, and give thanks when you find a glimpse, no matter whether it sounds like a riot in the wee hours of the morning, or smells pretty fishy.

PART FOUR

ROAD TO RECONCILIATION

Telling Our Story

Houston, Texas, USA
Union of Black Episcopalians Eucharist
Christ Church Cathedral

4 July 2007

The Union of Black Episcopalians had its origins in a racist and segregated church, and it continues a ministry of support and encouragement for African-Americans and Afro-Caribbeans in the Episcopal Church. Its annual gathering is an occasion of celebration and fellowship, and equipping for the work that is not yet finished.

Isaiah 42:1–7; Psalm 72:1–4, 12–14;
James 2:5–9, 12–17; Matthew 10:32–42

There is abundant irony in today's celebration, as this gathering calls for reconciliation on the day our nation gives thanks for freedom. It's sort of like talking about repentance at a wedding—but the reality is that reconciliation and freedom go hand in hand. That irony is a reminder of the eschatological hunger and reality of the gospel—freedom, reconciliation, and the reign of God are all around us and yet none of them is fully known or experienced.

We might start by remembering just what "reconciliation" means. If you take the word apart, it literally means "to call back together again." Or even, "to take counsel again, or to make friendly again." The word conveys an obvious sense of restoring what has been separated, and that ought to remind us of what it is we understand as God's mission, in which the church shares: to restore all people to unity with God and one another in Christ.

We live in a world that is not yet whole, and we understand our vocation as the healing or repair of that world—what our Jewish brothers and sisters call *tikkun olam*. We take on that vocation and attitude toward the world in baptism, when we say over and over again that we will respect the dignity of every human being, that we will seek and serve Christ in all others, and that we will strive for justice and peace. We promise as well to keep turning back toward God when we discover that we've turned away. Our promise to keep praying and meeting for worship is about being continually formed in that vocation of healing, repairing, and reconciling.

A healed world is the ancient dream of our tradition. That is what Isaiah speaks about so powerfully—that the servant of God will be a bringer of justice, a light to the nations, a healer of illness, and an emptier of prisons. Over and over and over again the prophets rail against those who bring greater division in the world, those who bring greater injustice and whose deeds sow destruction. And the prophets also bring hope and comfort to those who know that the world is not as it should be. That hope and comfort—literally, strengthening—is offered so that we can get out there and get busy.

We labor for many kinds of reconciliation—between individuals, within families, between and within nations, between political and even theological factions, between human beings and the rest of creation. In the largest sense, we labor for healing of all manner of injustice and want in this world. God's mission includes the mending of all of those wounds, and the world will not be whole until new flesh has grown in their place.

Healing begins when we describe the wound by telling our stories. We claim relationship with the God who hears the cries of the oppressed, the wanderers in the wilderness, and those who have no helper. Those cries and laments are the beginning of salvation, even though it may not always feel that way. The prayer of complaint about the "not yet" and our ability to speak that prayer remind us that something better is possible. That telling in prayer is like the remembering we do at Eucharist—this is what has been done, and we know that God has work for us to do as a result. God invites us to share in the work of healing the world.

The reconciliation we labor toward runs through every part of our lives. We all share the experience of being individuals who are separated from others. Recognizing that separation is the beginning of lament that can build solidarity once again. I can only speak out of my own experience, but in the ways in which that experience has parallels with others, together we can begin to build connections with one another. Let me offer an example. I know what it is to be marginalized because of my gender, even though I enjoy plenty of privileges in other ways. Yesterday on the way down here I ended up sitting next to a forty-something man on the airplane. He got up at some point and started to rummage around in the overhead bin. He'd been leaning over me and doing this for several minutes. I finally stood up to see what was going on, and saw that he was fussing with my bag. When I objected, he pulled my bag out and set it on the floor. Then he pulled his own bag down and put it in my seat, and then loudly accused me of having an attitude.

As a woman, I know what it is to be expected to comply or be quiet or not complain. And I have grown accustomed to resistance when I ask for and expect basic dignity, or the justice of equal treatment. My encounter was a very small incident, but it says something about privilege and its expectations. I don't think my traveling companion would have treated a man in the same way.

Why is loving our neighbors such hard work? When Jesus says, "Do not think that I have come to bring peace to the earth; I have not come to bring peace, but a sword" (Matt 10:34), he is at least in part talking about the kind of resistance that comes from challenging the injustice in this world. You and I are going to increase the division in this world, and we are going to discover that our near neighbors may be set against us when we begin to stir things up by asking hard questions and insisting on justice.

What hard stories need to be told here—today, or in this gathering, or here in Houston? Some of them, I know, have been told for centuries but still need telling and re-telling. Once those stories have been told and shared, what moves the lament toward healing?

The lament needs to be heard, and some sacramental act is needed in response. It's no different than what we ask in confession—telling the story to someone who can truly hear it, and then some outward sign that the pain has been acknowledged and a movement toward healing begun. That outward sign is what we're looking for—the outward and visible sign of an inward and spiritual healing given by the grace of God. In the case of my airplane encounter, my attempt was rebuffed. When I said, "I'm sorry you're having a bad day," my words were heard as rejection—and I can't deny that there might have been some there! Something more was obviously needed, but we two strangers weren't able to find it.

The kind of reconciliation that we are seeking in this church needs the same kind of sacramental sign—one that will be valued and accepted and seen as good faith toward healing. I have no personal knowledge of it, but I am told that the Episcopal Church's Special Convention in 1969 was understood and experienced in that way by some, and although it did not finish the work, it may have begun some healing—it was called in response to the urban riots, and sought to provide a financial demonstration of repentance for racism.

To achieve justice and reconciliation in this church we need a good deal more telling of stories, and ears and hearts to hear them. And having once heard, a concrete and sacramental response needs to follow. As James reminds us, "Faith by itself, if it has no works, is dead"(2:17). That concrete and sacramental response is what all marginalized people have asked for, throughout history. That is the cry in the wilderness—feed us, set us free, heal us, give us a home. Gay and lesbian Christians in this church are asking for full and sacramental recognition. Native Americans are asking for a response that has to do with their ancient connection to the land. Descendants of the African diaspora are asking for reparative justice after centuries of exploitation. Women continue to ask for full inclusion in the human race. Immigrants are asking for the freedom to live as equal citizens whose labor and dignity and full humanity are honored and valued. Even the dominant ones in our society need to be redeemed as human beings whose value does not depend on superior status. When one is oppressed, all are oppressed, and demeaned, and made less than they were created to be.

None of us can live in that kingdom God has promised until every single one of us is valued as beloved of God, not until each one of us has the sacramental evidence of that—in the outward and visible sign of a society of justice, where all have equal access to the blessings for which we were created, where ancient wounds have been salved, ancient dis-ease healed, and ancient injustice repaired.

When I looked up a bit of history about that Convention in 1969, I found Father Junius Carter's telling words: "Too long, bishops, you have sat on the sidelines and have not acted as our pastors! I urge you to intervene at this convention and exercise the authority that has been given you by our Lord."

We live in a somewhat less clerical time, and we are claiming the authority we have all been given at baptism. Nevertheless, all of us are meant to intervene as Father Carter implored—to jump in and tell the stories of lament and the stories of joy, to jump in and act in outward and visible ways, to be sacrament of reconciliation. Then and only then will we all be truly and finally free.

Through Justice to Reconciliation

New York, New York, USA
Tutu Center Dedication

12 September 2007

The Desmond Tutu Center is located at General Seminary, and dedicated to the work of reconciliation. The retired Archbishop was present for the opening, and we continue to delight in his ministry as chief Anglican prophet and imp. This address was one of several on the theme of reconciliation.

Reconciliation is God's mission—reconciling the world to God in Christ is the way Episcopalians put it. Reconciliation means restoring God's intention for the world. It's needed in the relationships between human beings and their creator, between and among human beings, and—in ways of which we are becoming increasingly aware—between human beings and the rest of creation.

The need for reconciliation comes from a violation of created order, which is the result of violence. Those words—"violation" and "violence"—mean the use of force. Their root lies in the word *vis*, which might be appropriately translated as vital force. Violence is the forcible use of one's life to impose one's will on another. It is the wrong and idolatrous use of the basic gift of life—the sinful use of spirit-breath. Reconciliation is the recovery of the right relationship to that basic gift of life. We might speak of it as a revivifying, a re-inspiration, or even the resurrection of a bond that has had the life sucked out of it. Where violence is the diminishment of another's life—and one's own in the process—reconciliation restores life, and even makes it richer. Jesus said, "I came that you might have life, and have it abundantly." Reconciliation is sacrament—outward sign—of life abundant.

The central focus of our faith, our proclamation of the resurrection, is about God's ultimate renewal and restoration of that gift of life. We proclaim the message that God's gift of life is more powerful than the world's misuse of it in violence, even the ultimate violence of execution.

If we think of reconciliation as sacrament, then it needs stuff or matter to do its work; words or intent alone are not adequate. The sacramental matter of reconciled relationship is what we call justice. It is the outward and visible sign of an inward, renewed, and grace-filled life. When we understand that the need for reconciliation is rooted in violence, we understand that the kind of justice we must seek must be restorative, not retributive. Retributive justice is intrinsically violent—it merely displaces the violence that produced a need for reconciliation. For example, much of our civil legal system, particularly capital punishment, depends on a philosophical and theological perspective that sees violence as the necessary response to profoundly violated relationships. By requiring payment with a life, that perspective holds that justice—in the sense of balance and fairness—is restored. Yet we rarely see more abundant life as the result.

Restorative justice, on the other hand, seeks to recover God's dream for creation through the repudiation of violence. The gift of life is meant to produce more life, rather than diminish it. Reconciliation, understood as restorative justice, seeks healing and longs for the wholeness of the original vision of the created order. In a very real sense, reconciliation seeks to restore the holiness for which creation was intended.

The prophets of our tradition, both the writing prophets like Isaiah, Micah, and Amos, and the latter-day prophets like Martin Luther King and Desmond Tutu, have always held up the well-being of the whole person, and the well-being of the whole community, as profoundly interconnected. Our tradition has always had at least a minor strand that affirms the place of the rest of creation in the final dream of God for a restored creation. We have more lately begun to recognize this as a larger community of faith. The theology of ubuntu, which Archbishop Tutu has proclaimed so tirelessly, insists that until all are healed, none can be. Until justice rolls down like waters and righteousness like an ever-flowing stream, God is not properly worshiped nor neighbor loved (Amos 5:24).

When that justice does roll down, what does it look like? Someone labeled this address "Through Justice to Reconciliation: Bearing Fruit on the Ground." And while perhaps the word order should have been different—"reconciliation through justice: bearing fruit on the ground"—the point should be evident. Without reconciliation, at least in its sacramental sense, there is no justice. The means of restorative justice, particularly the kind of justice that can bring a holy and life-giving renewal of relationship—the evidence of God at work "with skin on"—has to do with doing something concrete.

Bearing fruit on the ground implies an active participation in the work of justice-making. You and I, and the communities in which we have a part (and that means all of creation, not just human beings) have work to do. Looking at this through the lens of the more particular exercise of sacramental confession, this would be the penance part. But that word is so freighted with retributive overtones that it may not be helpful. Originally, penance was understood as the work required to both signify and begin to live an amended life. That is the sense in which we are all called to bear fruit.

Bearing fruit looks like building the reign of God. It looks like the pragmatic work of wiping runny noses, cleaning Aegean stables, and insisting that our warring siblings cease their name-calling and grenade-tossing. It is household work, both domestic and economic, for it has to do with cleaning up this *oikos,* this home in which all of us dwell. It is also political work, the work of building community. And in that sense of household work, we must get down on the ground—maybe even on our knees—and get our hands dirty. This work is about the ground zero where we live, both particularly and generally, here in Chelsea and on planet Earth.

Bearing fruit *is* dirty work, because this world is a mess—and who does God have to do that dirty work but us? But it is also the work for which we were created, as creatures made of the earth. Reconciliation is the work of *Adham*, it is our vocation. We will be more productive, and more able to respond to that vocation in holy and life-giving ways, if we can remember our origins. We are dust, and to dust we shall return—*and* we have been created only slightly lower than the angels. This is humble—literally earthy—work, *and* it is the most glorious occupation conceivable. We will find God, and be found by God, in this pursuit.

We cannot bear fruit without being ready to bear fruit, without being at least reasonably mature. The seedling vine or sapling fruit tree is incapable of it. When Jesus says "be perfect as your heavenly father is perfect," that is at least part of what he's talking about. Be whole, be mature, or at least well on the road toward maturity! For most of us, that means continually dealing with that old basic sin of idolatry—putting ourselves in the center of things—*will you persevere in resisting evil?* We can't bear the fruit of reconciled justice until we get out of our own way, until we recognize, way down in the life-giving core of our being—in the ground of our being—that the essence of life is about the whole of it, that until the whole world is reconciled, none of us will be, that until all the hungry are fed, we're not finished, that our own ultimate salvation depends on the free and full flourishing of all the rest of creation. In other words, we cannot save ourselves. We can only participate in God's mission to save the whole world.

What does God's mission look like? An awful lot of the prophetic imagination has to do with justice in the lives of the poor, the alien and the outcast, the victims of war, and those with no helper. That great eschatological dream is about enough to eat, and enough for feasting. It's about living without fear of soldiers or domestic violence. It's about care when you're sick. It's about every human being—and indeed all of creation—being treated with the dignity God sees in each. Human beings dream those great and ultimate dreams, through God's spirit, and we work at achieving them through the pragmatic and political, through concrete objectives like the Millennium Development Goals.

Okay. Let's get down and dirty. Six billion people, more or less, on this earth. Half of them live on less than $2 a day.[21] One billion live on less than $1 a day,[22] and most of them are starving. Hardly the heavenly banquet. A little more than a year ago, this church said that we would focus our work of reconciliation around a vision of a healed world that looks more like Isaiah's heavenly feast. We said that we would focus on the Millennium Development Goals as an image of what the reign of God looks like. We are doing that because we understand the MDGs as a sacrament of justice. Not the full monty, but an excellent start.

There are people out there, mostly church members, who haven't yet recognized the parallels, who ask why the church focuses on this when social service agencies and governments are better equipped to do the work. But the reason is quite simple, and it's profoundly important: we are focused on the MDGs because their achievement seems to be the best global example of what the reign of God could look like in our own day. It is a twenty-first-century version of what Jesus meant when he walked into the synagogue in Nazareth, read from Isaiah about preaching good news to the poor, feeding the hungry, and healing the sick, and announced, "Today this scripture has been fulfilled in your hearing."

The MDGs don't use overtly theological language to talk about feeding the hungry and educating children and seeing that people don't die from lack of medical care, but they do address the violence that separates one-third of humanity from the most basic things they need for "life abundant." If we are serious about the incarnation, then all of human existence is meant to be redeemed, healed, and restored to the state of wholeness for which we were created. When one part of the body suffers, all are diminished.

The world is not reconciled as long as some live without—without food, good news, adequate housing, peace, clothing, education, or justice. The work of this Church is to build a world of shalom that includes all those versions of God's dream—adequate food, drink, housing, employment, health care, education, equality, and the peace that comes only when true justice is present and available to all.

The Millennium Development Goals focus on extreme poverty—the kind of poverty that prevents children from developing their mental capacity fully because their bodies and brains are malnourished, and the kind of poverty that cuts people down in the prime of life and makes them far more susceptible to disease. The goals begin with the fact that a large fraction of the world's people do not have adequate caloric intake—and then seek to cut that rate in half by the year 2015. The other goals move on to include remedying some of the physical consequences of poverty—poor health and sanitation, lack of education, the interrelated environmental causes and consequences of poverty, and the economic and debt systems that keep people in poverty. Many of the goals focus on the *anawim*, the little ones on whom Jesus' own ministry focused—widows, orphans, those with infirmities and communicable diseases, women in general, those outcastes who labored at occupations deemed unclean. Like the healing work of Jesus, the MDGs seek to restore human beings to fully human community.

The first of the goals includes a commitment to cut the worst hunger and poverty in half by 2015. Radical poverty and malnutrition mean that most of those one billion hungry people are slowly starving. Each day, nearly fifty thousand people die because of poverty, and most are women and children.[23] At the same time, the three richest people in the world control more wealth than the 600 million living in the world's poorest countries.[24]

The second goal is to achieve universal primary education. Nearly a hundred million children are not in school, and in the poorest countries nearly half of the girls do not attend. Illiteracy rates for women in the poorest countries are twice as high as for men. Yet those with a primary education are less than half as likely to contract HIV. Universal primary education would cost $10 billion a year—less than half of what the U.S. spends each year on ice cream.[25]

The third goal is about women's equality and empowerment. When we begin to look at the complexion of this kind of radical poverty, we discover that it is mostly women and their children who are starving and living in penury, around the world and here at home. Across the globe, women do two-thirds of the work, produce half of the food, receive only 10 percent of the income, and own only 1 percent of the property.[26] Sociologists and development specialists have shown us repeatedly that when women are empowered and begin to enjoy some degree of autonomy, their families and communities begin to be transformed.

The fourth goal is to reduce childhood mortality and disease by two-thirds. Newborn mortality in Africa is at least forty-five per thousand; in developed nations, it's about five per thousand. Every three seconds a child in the developing world dies from treatable or preventable disease. Every day in sub-Saharan Africa, three thousand children under the age of five die of malaria.[27] All of these goals are interrelated, and all of them disproportionately affect women and their children. When mothers are malnourished, they bear children less resistant to disease. All are more susceptible to disease when they are inadequately fed.

The fifth goal seeks to improve maternal health and reduce the maternal mortality rate by three-quarters. Every year five hundred thousand women die in pregnancy or childbirth—one every minute. In parts of Africa, the lifetime risk of death in pregnancy is 1 in 16. In the U.S., it's 1 in 3500.[28] One reason is that in Africa, only about a quarter of births are attended by trained health workers. Malnutrition and disease also contribute to the burden.

The sixth goal is to reduce the incidence of preventable disease, such as HIV, malaria, and tuberculosis. Half the world's population lives in areas affected by malaria, and it kills between one and three million people annually. Tuberculosis kills another two million, and AIDS kills another two to three million. Thirty million people in Africa are HIV-positive, which represents 70 percent of all HIV infections in the entire world. In Zambia, 12 percent of children are AIDS orphans, and the number of orphans is growing in most parts of Africa.[29] As a global community, we spend about a quarter of what is necessary to treat and prevent AIDS. Once again, basic health status and educational levels are intimately related to infection rates and death rates from all these diseases.

The seventh goal has to do with environmentally sustainable development, especially providing clean water and adequate sanitation, and improving the conditions in slums. One billion people lack access to safe drinking water and 2.4 billion lack adequate sanitation, and every year 2 million children die as a direct result.[30] Two billion don't have regular access to clean and adequate energy, which contributes to the clearing of forests, and the use of fuels like kerosene, which are significant sources of pollution.

The last goal has to do with building global partnerships through fair trade rules, debt reduction, technology transfer, and enlightened drug policies. You may remember the major initiative for debt forgiveness in the developing world in the jubilee year of 2000. But today, 85 percent of that debt remains to be forgiven. In many cases, the amounts developing nations pay for debt service are far greater than what they have left to spend on health care, education, or other forms of development. The money spent on debt repayment each year could provide clean water for all. Cancellation of all developing world debt, over the course of twenty years, would cost each person in the developed nations a penny a day.[31] Would you be willing to contribute $3.65 a year?

The numbers involved are significant on one level, but trivial when the cost is considered in context. The European Union gives $86 billion in agricultural and trade subsidies every year. Five billion dollars could provide clean water and sanitation for everyone. The average cow in the EU gets $2 a day in subsidies; more than 3 billion people get by on that or less.[32] Changes in trade policies are also part this goal. Under current trade rules, a Mexican farmer who lives on $1 a day competes directly with a U.S. farmer who gets a $20K annual subsidy.[33] If developing countries got just 1 percent more of the export market, 128 million people would escape poverty.[34]

Let me simply say it again: All these goals are connected, and when they remain unrealized, the impact falls disproportionately on the poorest, particularly women and their children. Think for a moment about the interconnection between economy and ecology. The wealthy nations of the world are rapidly depleting the fishery stocks in many developing parts of the world. Bishop Packard tells me heart-rending stories about the Marshall Islands in the South Pacific, where factory trawlers come through and sweep the waters clean. The local subsistence fishers are close to starving. Those native peoples are also among the first who will lose their homeland as sea level begins to rise as a result of global warming.

Extractive approaches to resource use—like clear-cutting forests, and replacing the trees with cash crops for export, developing oil and gas without regard for local populations—these are the result of the injustices visited upon the peoples of many, many developing nations. Resource extraction like that is violent, for it sees resource only as what Martin Heidegger called *Bestand*, standing reserve— basically a commodity that is there only for my personal use. This way of thinking ignores and violates the fundamentally interconnected way in which all has been created.

How are we doing on these Goals? In most parts of the developing world we are falling far short. There are signs of hope, particularly around primary education and some indicators of health, but the sad reality is that most of the developed nations of the world have not yet begun to meet the fiscal commitments they made in 2000.

As the millennium began, 181 nations agreed to work at this kind of global healing. The developed nations agreed to help fund the reconciling work, with a fixed percentage of their annual national incomes. The developing nations committed themselves to fiscal transparency and working against corruption. Among the developed nations, only the Scandinavian countries, Luxembourg, and the Netherlands have met their promise. The numbers seem almost mind-numbingly large to some, yet in relative terms they are very small. The funds necessary to do this work are significant, yet represent less than 1 percent of the annual budgets of the world's developed nations.

Working toward the MDGs is a kind of evangelism. When we stand up and speak on behalf of God's dream, we are proclaiming that all people deserve good news. We can learn to tell others that as Christians, we believe that the world should not permit girls to be excluded from school or allow mothers to die in childbirth because no one will go and help. We believe that malaria is largely preventable, that all people should have clean water to drink and adequate food and shelter. We take seriously what Jesus says—that "whenever you did not do this to one of the least of these" you ignored the presence of God in your midst. Are we ready to live an amended life? It takes action. It takes a sacramental demonstration of our willingness to try.

You and I are meant to build a society of peace with justice, and we cannot do it without challenging the structures of this world, in all areas of human endeavor. Systems of injustice do not change only through silent prayer, though prayer is essential. Taking up our crosses daily means using all the gifts we have been given—the power of prayer (both silent and shouted from the housetops), the power of the vote, and the power of persuasion.

These are powerful tools indeed, and we can use them to hold out a vision of hope, and to help this country become reconcilers and healers rather than bearers of war and violence. It is long past time to beat our swords into plowshares, to lay down our weapons of destruction, and to build an open city of truly human relationships, rooted in the radical freedom and friendship of God.

The radical freedom of friendship with God is a gift that is often known by the poorest in this world. Those without the physical illusions of self-sufficiency know their dependence on God in a way that you and I rarely experience. That is something of what Jesus meant when he said the poor are blessed. It is also a stark reminder that the wealthy and developed parts of the world cannot march in and impose a development plan on the poorer and less developed parts of the world. Partnership is absolutely foundational, and a humble reminder that we are all profoundly interconnected. Each has gifts to give the other. One of the challenges for folks like you and me is that we have to learn to see the gifts of the poor. Let me urge you to go and do some uncomfortable work—some of that humble, dirty work. See and recognize the creativity and perseverance that's required to live on the streets, or feed a family on a food-stamp budget of a dollar a meal. You and I can do that work right here, and what we learn may make us far more effective advocates for those across the globe.

So what can we do, how can we participate in, this gospel work of healing the world? How can we bear fruit on the ground? Use your imagination—there are myriad ways. We can help fund the work through agencies like Episcopal Relief and Development, which understand the essential nature of seeing and empowering the gifts already present among the poor. We can spend our money and vacation time to go and partner with those on the margins—we can quite literally build the reign of God, one decent house and one school and one hospital at a time. We can pester our legislators, let them know how important we believe this work is—and keep on bothering them! Prayer is also an essential part of the dreaming and visioning that says a reconciled world is possible. Put on your thinking caps. Then put on your overalls.

May God bless the work, may God bless each of you, and may God bless our ability to continue to dream the dream of shalom and an entire creation restored.

Traveling Light

New Orleans, Louisiana, USA
Christ Church Cathedral
Feast of Philander Chase
23 September 2007

A visit to the diocesan cathedral during a meeting of the Episcopal bishops in New Orleans was an opportunity to celebrate the ongoing recovery from the devastation of hurricanes in 2005, particularly the recovery of the artistic gifts of this culturally blessed city.

Isaiah 44:1–6,8; Psalm 108:1–6; Acts 1:1–9; Luke 9:1–6

When I first heard about dedicating a trumpet at this service, I have to admit that I thought that we were going to dedicate a brace of organ pipes—those great big, bright and deep-throated ones that are often set over the doors to a church. It was a delight to discover that the trumpet we are going to bless today is one that will be carried out into the world, to breathe new life and spirit wherever it and its gifted player travel. The golden voice of this Elysian trumpet is a memorial to the dead—both Irvin Mayfield, Sr. and all those who died in Hurricane Katrina—but its work is to proclaim life, to sing of grief and to claim the ultimate victory of life over death. It is a tool for proclaiming the gospel in the multiple variations of jazz.

We're also remembering this morning the feast of another fallen saint—Philander Chase. Priest, bishop, founder of schools and churches, he was also often caught up in the storms of the religious system we call the Episcopal Church and its mother in the Church of England. His name means "lover," and we might most appropriately call him a lover in motion.

This morning's gospel has Jesus sending his disciples out to move around, bringing hope and healing wherever they go. He charges them to drive out division and heal. Proclaiming the kingdom of God is about reconciling the world; driving out demons is about removing all the forces that seek to divide—and both are essential kinds of healing. Those who are sent out get quite direct and simple instructions—travel light—and some other, more puzzling instructions, about entering and leaving houses and towns.

The people of this city had little choice about traveling light as they tried to flee the winds and waters of Katrina. Some got out early enough to take a suitcase and drive away for what they thought would be a weekend. They returned to find that everything they knew was gone. Suddenly they were traveling lighter than they ever would have chosen. Others who were unable to leave so early swam down streets with nothing but the clothes on their backs.

Yet those forced to travel light, or even start over with nothing, can find grace along the way when something or someone connects them with what they knew of home. Yesterday I heard two stories about precious things lost from churches during Hurricane Camille in 1969—one a statue of Mary recovered from the mud after the storm and a source of solace through the years since. It was packed carefully and taken away before Katrina came, and it is still bringing a sense of connection with the home people once knew. The other was a silver box for keeping consecrated bread, lost after Camille, but discovered again a couple of miles away, washed up out of the bay after Katrina. Both have brought a measure of comfort to grieving congregations—gifts of light and peace in the midst of unencumbered— and unchosen—traveling.

This trumpet we will bless today is hardly light, yet the sacrificial gifts that have made it possible are a sacramental expression of others' ability to travel a bit lighter, both for those who have given and those who will receive. This instrument is going to travel all over this land, and it's going to trumpet forth good news and healing for those who have been lost. It will cry out, "Come join this line, find a home here, and know you're not alone. The God who gives us breath is going to sing the jazz of life in you once more."

Traveling light can be a wrenching grief when it is forced and not chosen. Yet it can also hold the seeds of grace. And it is toward that possibility that the gospel words about houses and towns are meant to lead us. "Whatever house you enter, stay there—and leave from there" (9:4). When Luke reports Jesus giving similar instructions to the seventy a chapter later, he seems to warn against running about from house to house, looking for a more comfortable bed or a better meal. But here Luke seems to say quite the opposite: "Keep on moving." Yes, go in and stay a while, he seems to imply, but don't get too comfortable—you'll be on your way again before too long.

I heard a woman yesterday tell her evacuation story about trying nine different shelters before she finally found a place that could help, a place that could welcome her and begin to heal the disease of "no place at all." She is settling once again, healing, and in turn being a source of healing to others. Many of you here have had the experience of helping to heal a house that has been lost—gutting, painting, putting on a roof—so that it may once again become a home, so that those who were lost may once more enter and remain and go forth again from an earthly home.

Irvin Mayfield's memorial trumpet is going out there, into lots of different houses, to sing good news and begin to heal the disease of grief and loss and not knowing a home anyplace at all. And then this trumpet of resurrection is going to move on to another house and do the same work again.

Philander Chase kept on moving, too. He started in New Hampshire, went to New York to study to be a priest, traveled all over western New York planting churches, and settled in Poughkeepsie, New York, on the banks of the Hudson River. He stayed there six years, and then came here to New Orleans to start this congregation in 1805. Again he stayed only six years before he took off again, this time heading back east to Connecticut. Six more years there, then off to Ohio to start a school. Not long after, he was named bishop of Ohio, and two years later, president of Cincinnati College. Since there weren't enough trained clergy, he decided to found a theological college, and went to England to raise funds. At the same time his plans managed to ruffle the feathers of the Eastern establishment, who believed that that the seminary in New York should be more than adequate. His efforts produced Kenyon College, but his methods produced a lot of resistance. So he brushed off the dust and resigned both as bishop and president of Kenyon in 1831. This time he was off to Michigan, but four years later he was surprised to find himself elected bishop of Illinois, even before that diocese was formally recognized (more ruffled feathers—and canons!). He moved to Peoria, laid plans to start another seminary, went to England again to raise money, and Jubilee College was born in 1839. He became the senior and presiding bishop in 1843.

Philander Chase died in 1852 as he lived, on the road. An expert at traveling light, he was an itinerant lover of God and fellow human beings, sure that the gospel meant not only establishing worshiping communities, but educational institutions that could teach good news, both theological and practical.

So what does it take for us to travel light? Well, it takes less than we may think we need—after all, the signs of new life here in New Orleans are the result of many people discovering they can live with less by sharing their abundance or letting go of unimportant things.

But it does take more than nothing at all, to judge the grief that is so widespread. If we ourselves are to be trumpeters of good news, banishers of disease and division, and proclaimers of the presence of God in our midst, we have to know something of home and community. We have to know we belong to somebody else, that some people care enough for us to work for our well-being and to help us sing lament, express our grief, and get in line. This parade that's forming is going to dance to the beat of good news, but it needs all of us in the line, not just those of us here this morning. It needs every other human being on this planet—black, white, brown; it needs the poor, the destitute, and those with more than enough to share; it needs the grieving, the ill, and those who know the blessing of restored health. This procession is going down to the grave, and it's going to dance away on the other side, but only when we join the traveling throng. None of us is going home until all of us have a place to lay our heads, and music for our grieving hearts, and a feast for the belly and for the soul. When the saints go marching in, it's going to be with every last one of us.

Thanksgiving

Guam
Thanksgiving
21–22 November 2007

The presiding bishop has responsibility for the Episcopal churches in Micronesia—
Guam and Saipan at present, although the Bishop for Chaplaincies does almost all of
the pastoral work. It had been about thirty years since a presiding bishop had visited,
but the welcome I received will, I hope, lead me back much sooner. These isolated
islands are communities of great hospitality.

Deuteronomy 8:1–3, 6–10; Psalm 65:9–14;
James 1:17–18, 21–27; Matthew 6:25–33

I was in North Korea last Thursday. It was cold and rainy, and it even started snowing as we hiked up a beautiful mountain. We were there with a delegation from South Korea, Japan, and Australia to share some aid and assistance with a village that had been devastated by floods last summer. We saw a place filled with profound beauty, particularly once the snow and rain stopped. But we also saw a pinched place—poor and cold and lacking many of the freedoms we take for granted.

After waiting all day for official permission to meet representatives of the village, we finally joined them in the yard of the local Hyundai office. We had sent ahead several pallets of dry cement mix, a number of packages of plastic greenhouse covers, and several boxes of medical supplies. We gathered in the rain to greet each other, and to give thanks for the opportunity to meet our neighbors—and to communicate haltingly through our South Korean hosts. But there was laughter amid the awkwardness, and I went away profoundly grateful for the opportunity to be in a place that Americans have often seen only as enemy territory. I gave thanks for the ability to see the need of people who are our neighbors, even though they are far away, and living behind a big and ferocious fence. And I give thanks for the very tentative beginnings of a relationship, a relationship begun and nurtured by the Anglican Church of South Korea.

The land of abundance that Deuteronomy paints for us, that land filled with grain and fruit, "where you may eat bread without scarcity" (8:9), is what God intends for each of us. This Thanksgiving feast is both a present reminder of the abundance we enjoy, and a reminder of the dream God has for all of our sisters and brothers. When James says in his letter that pure religion is about caring for orphans and widows, he is talking about the work we do to make sure that all our neighbors enjoy that kind of abundance.

I saw a powerful example of this in South Korea. On Sunday we visited a gathering of the faithful at a place called a "sharing house." It is an intentional gathering of rich and poor in a small house, where people come together to share their lives, to worship together, to feed one another, and to be fed. Those who have abundance in the world's terms share that abundance. Those who have little share their presence and the gift of receiving. This faith community, and a number of others like it, has given birth to several other ministries of sharing. One is a shelter for teenaged boys, another is a shelter for homeless families. There is a training program for the mentally disabled, an after-school tutoring program, a girls' shelter, a counseling center, and a ministry to lonely seniors. All of these services have grown out of this small worshipping community, from a sense of thanksgiving for what they have and what they can share with others. This congregation of seventy-five or so people is transforming a much larger community through its focus on abundance. It is an example of what Jesus means when he tells his followers not to worry about what they're going to eat or drink or wear. If they focus first on that dream of God for an abundant community, they will find themselves living in abundance.

What abundance are you grateful for this year? Your family, your health, your safety? For a new job, new relationships? For children, grandchildren, friends? For a new skill or ability? The urge to give thanks is the most basic religious response. That "religion, pure and undefiled" that James talks about begins in gratitude. And it's not just limited to the great and wonderful things that are easy to be grateful for. It's also possible to be thankful for the tough things in life—the losses and the pain and suffering. At some point, finding the blessing in the dark places redeems those challenges. Finding the blessing there is the source of true joy. It's taking seriously the reality that God is the source of all blessings. It's trusting radically in God.

This feast we call Thanksgiving is both a secular holiday and a religious one. We give thanks as Christians every time we gather—and in fact "Eucharist" means thanksgiving. But this yearly feast is especially a reminder to give thanks in the hard times.

Our civic holiday has its roots in the Civil War. Abraham Lincoln appointed the fourth Thursday in October as a national day of Thanksgiving in 1863, in the closing months of that war. He was in a lonely and grief-stricken position, facing a tough reelection struggle. He knew that if he lost, the country would surely become two nations as the Confederate states departed from the union. Members of his cabinet were mocking him in public. His wife had just been investigated as a traitor. The Union had won only one small battle in its long war with the southern states. Most people would have understood a bitter and angry explosion from him in that dark day. But his response instead was to appoint a national day of Thanksgiving, a time to remember the source of all our blessings, whether the times seem good or bad.

Jesus encourages us to give thanks for our blessings without worrying about where the next blessing will come from. If the birds and the lilies are cared for by a gracious creator, won't God care even more for human creatures? Some people think this means that nothing bad should ever happen to us. But what about those birds of the air? Some are electrocuted by power lines. Some are killed in collisions with cars on the highway. Around here, many are eaten by brown tree snakes. And no bird lives very long. Does that mean God doesn't care for them?

And those lilies—what about them? Usually all we pay attention to are the glorious and fragrant blooms. But that glory is only a small part of the lily's life. After the bloom fades, the greenery lasts a time, and then it too dies and fades away. But the lily continues as a brownish lump below the ground. Think of a dry onion—that's what a lily looks like much of the year. This seeming death is as much a part of the blessing of being a lily as the festive flower of Easter. Should we give thanks only for the bloom? Can we also give thanks for the fullness of the lily's life?

I've heard people here tell me repeatedly about the blessings of typhoons—buildings are renovated and communities come back stronger than they were before.

Thanksgiving is about learning the art of giving thanks even in hard times, in dark times, in times that try the soul. That ability to give thanks in the midst of darkness—and especially the ability to share that thanksgiving—gives rise to joy. Like the lily bulb buried in the ground, thanksgiving is what lets us take in sustenance, even when the world looks bleakest. Joy comes from the assurance that God is with us, sustaining us and blessing us, even if the world thinks we're done for.

Our ability to laugh last Thursday in North Korea, after a long day of waiting around and twiddling our thumbs, had something to do with finding the blessing in the midst of stress and struggle. Our ability to greet former enemies with joy, and their ability to greet us, even tentatively, has something to do with finding blessing even in the midst of want and oppression. The full and abundant joy of the sharing house that we visited in Korea has to do with the ability to bless and give thanks for all who gather—the homeless, the disabled, the lonely elders—to give thanks and insist that together, as we share the abundance we know, we are in the presence of God. I gather that something very like it happens here at St. Paul's on Saipan.

What do you give thanks for this year? And where will your thanks-giving let you share and spread abundance?

Saying Yes

Washington, DC, USA
Bolling Air Force Base, military and chaplains
21 December 2008

We had originally planned to visit chaplains in Iraq and Afghanistan, but we weren't able to go. The backup plan, which turned out to be a powerful blessing, was to visit chaplains in and around Washington, DC, at Walter Reed and the Episcopal worshipping community at the Pentagon.

4th Sunday of Advent: 2 Samuel 7:1–11, 16;
Luke 1:46–55; Romans 16:25–27; Luke 1:26–38

I've started twitching. I'm not used to being addressed as "ma'am." I know it's an important sign of recognizing authority in military culture, but it startles me every time I hear it—I'm usually turning around looking for my grandmother.

What happens when authority calls?

David, the military general, is now king, and thinks it's time to end the military campaign. David has been able to settle down, and act like peace really has come. He's even built himself a great palace, with pillars and beams made from those great cedars of Lebanon. So why should God's ark still be in a tent? He's acting with authority in that scene from 2 Samuel, and Nathan agrees with his strategy—until that night, when he has a dream. That dream reminds both Nathan and David who is the ultimate authority and strategist, the one with a view from above. To the offer of a permanent and palatial home, God basically says, "No thanks. I've been wandering around with these people from the very beginning; I'm not going to stop now. But I will build *you* a house, David—a dynasty that will last."

What happens when authority calls on Mary? Her encounter with the angelic messenger starts in an odd way. The usual opening line of an angel is, "Fear not!" but this one begins with a different salutation, "Greetings, favored one." Those words could also be translated, "Rejoice, blessed one." The angel might even be saying, "I salute you." Mary is startled by this unconventional opening, and the gospel says that she "pondered what sort of greeting this might be." What's going on here? This isn't a normal encounter between angel and mortal, and it's not a normal encounter between superior and subordinate. The angel's not saying, "Don't be afraid, the cavalry's on its way," or even, "Atten-hut! Here are your orders." The angel's opening a conversation—as if between equals.

The message *is* about orders, but in a different sense than you and I think about them. This isn't a military order, a command from a superior who expects immediate and almost unquestioning obedience. I know that military orders can be refused if the recipient believes them to be unlawful, but I also know that the consequences are pretty unpleasant, and you can't expect to use a defense of illegal orders and get off scot-free. There is absolutely no sense of forcible compulsion about the angel's order.

This conversation between Gabriel and Mary is about sharing a vision, the kind of perspective a general might have—the strategy of a *strategos*, the general who climbs up the hill to survey the battlefield. Gabriel is offering a big picture and asking if Mary will cooperate. Sort of like the old *Mission Impossible* opener "Your mission, should you choose to accept it. . . ." Mary is given a choice that she can accept or not. The *strategos* has other options if the answer is no.

Mary's first response is, "Sorry, unable, the equipment's not ready." But Gabriel is undeterred: "Doesn't matter," he replies. "Elizabeth thought the same thing. And she's six months into this deployment."

Mary's next response is remarkable. She says, "Here I am, ready to serve." And then, what's usually translated as "Let it be with me according to your word" actually starts out the same way a command does: "Let it be done." In Latin, it's *fiat*. She claims the authority offered her. She commands, in full cooperation with the one who has asked. She claims authority, and responds with authority.

The letter to the Romans suggests that Mary's fiat is "the obedience of faith." Mary hears, responds, and claims the authority to act. She doesn't mindlessly follow orders as though a gun's been put to her head, but she responds out of a deep conviction that this is God's call. This is what is sometimes called submission to God—putting yourself under orders out of faithfulness to God's larger mission.

I'm going to make a connection here that may challenge you, but it's an important link to God's larger mission. Mary is also revered by Muslims, who recognize her as a righteous woman, and deeply value her example of submission to the will of God. Muslims do not see her son as divine, but they do believe he was born to a virgin. The Koran actually mentions Mary more often than the New Testament does. The word *Islam* means submission to God, and Mary is revered because she is such an important example of what that looks like. That word *Islam* has the same root as *shalom* and *salaam*, words usually translated as "peace."

God's mission, the mission of the Prince of Peace, is about reconciling the world. The Christian story of that reconciling work begins with Mary.

In a very real sense, Mary is the first human being to make a Christian response. Her cooperation with that larger mission is at the root of Christianity. Faith in divine authority and claiming one's own authority to partner with God—the *strategos*—is part of our Christian life.

We're all people under authority. Clergy—deacons, priests, and bishops—are called "ordained" because we have taken vows (or accepted orders) to live a disciplined life, obeying the pastoral authority of others. All the baptized are under authority—at baptism we make solemn vows to give our hearts to God and live in particular ways that build up the body—both the body of our own existence and our existence in the community called the Body of Christ. Living an ordered existence is about discipline, practice, and *askesis*—a Greek word that means athletic training.

The ascetic practices of our faith tradition are about training for mission— God's mission to heal this world, to build a world of peace, with justice, for all. That's what all that prophetic language about building straight roads in the desert is about. That's what God has in mind for David and his dynasty—to build a society where no one goes to war anymore, where there isn't any more poverty or the violence that results, where everyone has the opportunity for meaningful work, and no one stays sick because he can't afford medical care. That's what the song of Mary is about—the one she sings after the angel visits:

> *"My soul proclaims the greatness of the Lord, for he has looked with favor on his lowly servant. The almighty has done great things for me; he has mercy on those who fear him, he has scattered the proud, cast down the mighty from their thrones, and lifted up the lowly. He has fed the hungry with good things, and sent the rich away empty."* (Luke 1:46–53)

Mary's "yes" is a choice to participate in God's work of healing the world. It's the same choice you and I get every day—to say "yes" to the free and open invitation to cooperate and co-create as part of the healing, redeeming work of God in Christ. It's not about taking orders simply because they are written down, or spoken, or demanded. It is about a careful and thoughtful and whole-hearted decision to participate. It is about claiming the authority God has given us.

"Let it be with me according to your word—according to the word you spoke in Jesus, and the word you spoke in creation. I choose those orders you spoke at the beginning of creation, and the word spoken again in Jesus, who comes among us to make creation new."

What's your response going to be the next time you hear God calling?

Notes

1. John Donne, "Meditation XVII," *Devotions Upon Emergent Occasions and Death's Duel* (New York: Vintage, 1999), 103.
2. An infectious disease caused by parasitic worms.
3. *The Salt Eaters* (New York: Vintage Books, 1981), 265.
4. http://www.philly.com/inquirer/front_page/A_personal_resurrection.html
5. http://www.chestnuthillumc.org/pastors.htm
6. Blessed are you, Adonai, our God, ruler of the universe.
7. Daniel Ladinsky, *Love Poems from God: Twelve Sacred Voices from the East and West* (New York: Penguin, 2002), 7.
8. Ladinsky, 100.
9. Ladinsky, 61.
10. James Russell Lowell, "Once to Every Man and Nation," *The Hymnal 1940 of the Protestant Episcopal Church in the U.S.A.* (New York: Church Pension Fund, 1943), hymn 519.
11. the service of ordination
12. New York: Ballantine Books, 2007.
13. Minneapolis: Augsburg Fortress Publishers, 2007.
14. *A Contemporary Genesis;* see http://www.healingourplanetearth.org/contemporary_genesis.htm
15. Psalm 33; a translation used at this service.
16. Intergovernmental Panel on Climate Change—3rd Assessment, Synthesis Report, Summary for Policy Makers: http://www.ipcc.ch/ipccreports/
17. *Collected Verse of Rudyard Kipling* (Cambridge: University Press, 1907), 285–287.
18. "Sea-Fever," *Salt-Water Ballads* (London: Elkin Mathews, 1913), 59.
19. Fiona Macleod (1855–1905), cited in Brendan O'Malley, *Celtic Blessings and Prayers* (Mystic, CT: Twenty-third Publications, 1998), 155.
20. David Adam, *The Open Gate* (Harrisburg, PA: Morehouse, 1995), 111.
21. "State of Food Insecurity in the World 2006" (Food and Agriculture Organization of the United Nations, 2006).
22. "World Development Indicators 2007" (The World Bank, March 2007).

23. Reality of Aid 2004 (Canada's Coalition to End Poverty—CCIC, 2004)/ World Health Organization 2004.

24. Share the World's Resources: http://www.stwr.org/poverty-inequality/ key-facts.html

25. ActionAid: www.actionaid.org

26. United Nations/WomenWatch: www.un.org/womenwatch

27. World Health Organization: http://www.who.int/features/factfiles/ malaria/en/index.html

28. United Nations: http://www.un.org/apps/news/story.asp?NewsID=12068& Cr=maternal&Cr1=

29. Global Health Facts: www.globalhealthfacts.org

30. UNICEF Sanitation Statistics: http://www.childinfo.org/areas/sanitation/

31. "Unfinished Business," Jubilee 2000 report: http://www.jubileeresearch .org/databank/usefulstatistics/generalstats.htm

32. American Enterprise Institute for Public Policy Research: http://www.aei .org/publications/pubID.17839/pub_detail.asp

33. "Is NAFTA Good for Mexico's Farmers?" CBS Evening News: http://www .cbsnews.com/stories/2006/07/01/eveningnews/main1773839.shtml

34. Market Trade Fair: http://www.maketradefair.com/assets/english/report_ english.pdf